CURRICULUM SIMPLEXITY

Are you a busy teacher, subject lead or senior leader looking to improve your curriculum? Based on the theory of simplexity, the idea that clarity and logic can make even the most complex tasks manageable, *Curriculum Simplexity* offers a practical and systematic planning aid, guiding readers through the process of building a robust, coherent whole-school curriculum. Recognising the role of teachers' autonomy and professional judgement, this essential read provides space for the flexibility and creativity needed for teachers to reflect their own values, content, aims and outcomes within the curriculum.

Divided into a series of easily digestible chapters and filled with templates, worked examples and planning formats, this book unpacks the process of creating a curriculum. Topics explored include, but are not limited to:

* The importance of pedagogy
* Good subject leadership
* Building a curriculum progression framework
* Implementing, delivering and evaluating your curriculum
* Assessment

Highly practical and written in an accessible style, teachers are encouraged to reflect on their curriculum planning, development and delivery. This is an essential read for any teacher, subject lead or senior leader who wishes to improve their curriculum and support positive learning outcomes within their school.

Melanie Moore is a highly experienced primary educator with over 30 years of experience working as a classroom teacher, Deputy Headteacher and curriculum leader. She has also worked for several years as primary curriculum advisor for Sheffield Education Authority and is founder and curriculum director of Cornerstones Education Ltd.

CURRICULUM SIMPLEXITY

A Practical Guide for Developing Your
Primary Curriculum

Melanie Moore

Routledge
Taylor & Francis Group

LONDON AND NEW YORK

Designed cover image: © Getty Images

First published 2025
by Routledge
4 Park Square, Milton Park, Abingdon, Oxon, OX14 4RN

and by Routledge
605 Third Avenue, New York, NY 10158

Routledge is an imprint of the Taylor & Francis Group, an informa business

© 2025 Melanie Moore

British Library Cataloguing-in-Publication Data
A catalogue record for this book is available from the British Library

ISBN: 978-1-032-78178-5 (hbk)
ISBN: 978-1-032-78179-2 (pbk)
ISBN: 978-1-003-48658-9 (ebk)

DOI: 10.4324/9781003486589

Typeset in Joanna MT Std
by codeMantra

CONTENTS

ACKNOWLEDGEMENTS

This book would not have been possible without the support and guidance of some extraordinary people. First, a huge thank you to Dr Fran Barnes who worked tirelessly to edit and proof all my drafts. Thank you also to Alex Wright for all your brilliant design work and attention to detail.

An especially big thank you to Dale French and Gill Quantrell, who offered the benefit of their experience and expertise on various aspects of this book and to my colleagues at Cornerstones Education — your support and encouragement are very much appreciated.

Finally, to my family and partner, Simon, thank you for your patience and support, as always.

PREFACE

Welcome!

Hello reader, and a warm welcome to my first book, *Curriculum Simplexity: A Practical Guide for Developing Your Primary Curriculum*. I hope it becomes a much-valued part of your curriculum journey.

About me

I am a curriculum geek. I adore the entire curriculum development process: the creativity, innovation and endless possibilities for building something that helps children thrive. I am passionate about primary education and have been a primary teacher, adviser and curriculum specialist for over 30 years. My company, Cornerstones Education, supports thousands of schools to build, develop and improve their curricula, and I love it. This book is a means of sharing my expertise and a celebration of those fantastic teachers and leaders I have had the privilege of working with on their curriculum journeys.

Challenging times

I know that the curriculum development process can feel complex and challenging. This is especially true for busy teachers and senior leaders already 'wearing many hats' in their day-to-day school life. Moreover, the challenges of curriculum development have been exacerbated further by the COVID-19 pandemic despite teachers and senior leaders working tirelessly throughout to negate any adverse effects. However, as most primary teachers and leaders already know, as they have seen it first-hand, children's academic attainment and well-being have suffered. Contrary to expectation, this appears to bear no specific relation to 'privilege or deprivation' (Ofsted).

Furthermore, other factors, such as budgetary restrictions, teacher shortages, lack of opportunities for continuing professional development and pressures from outside bodies such as the Office for Standards in Education (Ofsted) in England, continue to pressure primary schools.

With all these factors at play, how do we ensure the curriculum receives the attention it deserves? How do we give teachers and senior leaders the tools and materials to help children learn and become happy, confident and resilient individuals? What is needed is a straightforward, transparent process. One that acknowledges your challenges and tackles them head-on without overcomplication or unnecessary workload.

Curriculum Simplexity

So, this book is for you whether you want to improve or refresh your current curriculum or create something entirely new. By taking each stage of the curriculum development process and breaking them down into manageable and digestible chunks, this book ensures that whatever context you're in, or experience you have, your work will result in a tangible outcome. What's more, you'll find all the tasks, resources, and examples you need to get the job done between the pages of this handy book. This approach is Curriculum Simplexity.

Using this book

You and your school are unique. And so will your journey be throughout this book. How you use it depends on your school's starting point, your confidence, and your expertise. And because no two schools are the same, you can decide how to use the book, either following the process from start to finish or using it as a resource to dip in and out of, according to your needs. While many of the examples I use relate to the English national curriculum, with some tweaks and adaptations, the principles and process can apply to you wherever you are in the world.

Make the most of the advice and ideas and enjoy doing the suggested tasks with your team. Feel free to use and copy the templates, examples, and case studies included. They'll offer a good starting point for your discussions and help save you time.

Getting started

Finally, in all my years in primary education, one thing remains indisputable: the curriculum, when planned and taught well, is a powerful tool for improving children's academic and emotional well-being. It is also a fantastic vehicle for social justice. Whenever I walk into a school or classroom where the curriculum is planned and taught well, it is easy to feel its presence doing good.

So, before you begin, take a breath. Relax. Curriculum Simplexity is here to help. Look at the journey positively and enjoy the opportunity to create your unique and powerful primary curriculum.

References

Ofsted. Children hardest hit by the COVID-19 pandemic are regressing in basic skills and learning. Published Nov 2020. Accessed 12 February 2024. Ofsted: Children hardest hit by COVID-19 pandemic are regressing in basic skills and learning – GOV. UK (www.gov.uk)

(Unknown). Childhood Education Published 1924. Association for Childhood Education International. Simplexity is a neologism which suggests a complementary relationship between complexity and simplicity. The term was first published in the journal 'Childhood Education' (1924).

INTRODUCTION

THE CURRICULUM DEVELOPMENT PROCESS

What is curriculum development?

Curriculum development is often confused with curriculum design, but curriculum design is only part of a more extensive, holistic and continuous school improvement process. In this book, curriculum development refers to the systematic analysis, planning, designing, implementation and evaluation of your curriculum.

Leading the process

In most primary schools, curriculum development is typically undertaken by a combination of senior, subject and key stage leaders. Some schools appoint specific curriculum leaders to lead and manage the entire process. However, this phenomenon is relatively new and often relies on a healthy school budget. In the best instances, teachers and other stakeholders such as school governors, parents, carers and children are also involved. However,

DOI: 10.4324/9781003486589-1

this needs to be well-managed to avoid any complications or confusion, particularly around roles and responsibilities. Whatever your circumstance, all stakeholders must know who is leading the entire process. That does not mean that this person is responsible for doing all the work; it is right and fair to delegate. However, it does mean that when a school identifies some-one to oversee and lead the whole process, they have a much better chance of coherence across the school. Before starting your curriculum journey, it is essential to be clear on who is leading the process and the roles and responsibilities of others.

The case for simplification

Simplifying the complicated is not easy. Complexities must be very well understood before they can be simplified. Having encountered the com-plexities of curriculum development many times, my approach simplifies them effectively to enable you to access and understand them more easily. So, while some people thrive on the complexities of a problem, most of us prefer to discover the nub of the thing. Even the great master Da Vinci declared 'simplicity is the ultimate sophistication'.[1]

Amongst the benefits of presenting a process in its simplest form is that you can more easily digest the information; hence, the process becomes much more manageable and even enjoyable. That is not to say that the pro-cess is dumbed down or has lost its intellectual integrity, but that light is shed only on its essential components and not the more minor, irrelevant, or superficial aspects of the process.

Curriculum Development Wheel

The Curriculum Development Wheel, seen in Figure 0.1, outlines sim-plexity's four-phase curriculum development process. As mentioned in the previous paragraph, all stakeholders must understand this to ensure a collective buy-in and understanding.

Ideally, you should work through the phases sequentially. However, if you already understand your curriculum needs and are confident in your knowledge of broader curriculum issues, you may move straight to the goal-setting phase. Scan each chapter to get an overview of the entire

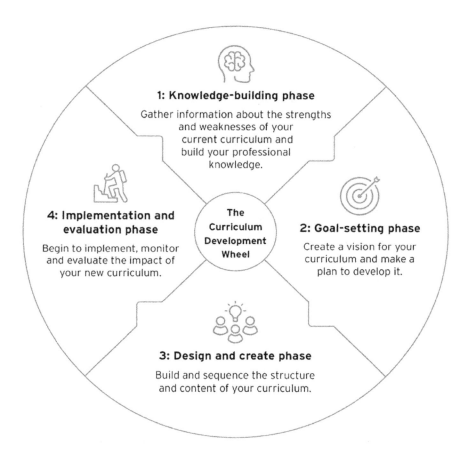

Figure 0.1 Curriculum Development Wheel.

process and what's involved before deciding where your school wants or needs to begin. It is important to note that while each phase has a specific focus, they are connected. As you work through the process, you can build on the work you have done in the previous phase. The aims of each phase are outlined in the following paragraphs.

Knowledge-building phase

The first phase of the curriculum development process will support you in gathering and analysing critical information about the strengths and weaknesses of your current curriculum. It will also provide you with opportunities to build your and your colleagues' professional knowledge around various issues concerning the curriculum. This knowledge-building phase includes chapters about different types of curricula, knowledge, the role of subject leaders, cultural capital, localisation, pedagogy and the component parts of a robust curriculum. Each chapter has a range of suggested practical tasks, examples, and questions to stimulate and focus your thinking. This phase generally takes about three months to complete, depending on the size and complexities of your school.

Goal-setting phase

During the second phase of the process, you can use the information you have gathered in Phase 1, to discuss and agree your curriculum goals. This phase includes two chapters, each with a range of tasks to help you set out the vision for your curriculum and then translate your vision into targeted objectives. These objectives will become the priorities of your curriculum development plan. This phase can take about a month to complete as you will already have begun to develop your ideas during the first phase.

Design and create phase

This third and most dynamic phase provides a sequenced set of practical tasks by which you can redesign your existing curriculum or create a new one. This phase includes opportunities to establish or revise the big ideas of your curriculum, identify the key concepts of each subject, build or strengthen your curriculum progression framework, create the subject narratives and topics of your curriculum, and curate the resources you need to teach and assess learning. This phase should involve all stakeholders and generally takes about 12–18 months.

Implementation and evaluation phase

In this final phase of the curriculum development process, you will begin implementing, monitoring and evaluating your new or improved curriculum.

Most importantly, this phase will give you and others necessary information about the impact and effectiveness of your changes and allow you to tweak and address any issues found in your monitoring, observations and evidence. You'll begin to see emerging areas of strength in your curriculum and identify gaps or misconceptions in what children know and can do. In turn, this will help you to identify areas for ongoing development.

You should expect it to take 6–12 months before you begin to see the impact of your curriculum, with some changes taking much longer to embed. As you build your knowledge of what is and is not working, you will naturally return to the first phase.

Curriculum terminology

As you embark on the development process, it is crucial to establish a common vocabulary amongst all stakeholders. A shared lexicon will simplify your discussions, debates and decision-making, as everybody has the linguistic tools to engage in deeper, more focused professional dialogue. A glossary of terms used in this book is provided to support you in achieving a shared vocabulary.

Summary

Improving or developing any curriculum is an ongoing process that demands time, resilience and dedication. It can also require imagination, innovation and social and emotional skills, especially when working with diverse groups of stakeholders. Even the most experienced curriculum developers rarely find the process plain sailing, even when it is simplified.

The phrase 'painting the Forth Bridge' is often used to describe the curriculum development process. When we think we have reached the end of it, we realise we need to go back to the start. And it is true – curriculum development is a cyclical process, not a means to an end.

Trust the process in this book; your work will bring its own rewards. By the end of it, you can have a much-strengthened curriculum or something completely new and exciting. Either way, this work is a privilege. An opportunity to expand children's minds and shape their futures.

Note

[1]   Leonardo da Vinci > Quotes > Quotable Quote. Goodreads. Accessed 12 February 2024. https://www.goodreads.com/quotes/9010638-simplicity-is-the-ultimate-sophistication-when-once-you-have-tasted

Reference

Da Vinci, Leonardo di ser Piero – (15 April 1452–2 May 1519).

PHASE 1: SYNOPSIS

THE KNOWLEDGE-BUILDING PHASE

In this first phase of the book, you can refresh or update your professional knowledge of different types of curricula, knowledge, the role of subject leaders, cultural capital, curriculum localisation, pedagogy and the component parts of a robust curriculum. Each chapter provides you with various practical tasks to do individually or with colleagues. The activities will help you reflect upon your existing curriculum and form ideas about what you want for a new or improved curriculum. You can decide which tasks are appropriate for you and your school and which will help you to develop your curriculum best.

As you progress through this phase, I recommend recording your thoughts, ideas and findings, as this will help you organise your priorities for the second phase of the process.

DOI: 10.4324/9781003486589-2

1

DEFINING THE CURRICULUM

Most teachers understand the curriculum as the academic concepts, skills and knowledge they want their children to learn. To some, it can also include the 'other stuff' children encounter during the day, such as assemblies, story time and constructive play. So, if you were to ask your colleagues to define the curriculum, you would likely receive a range of different responses. This is because the curriculum can often mean different things to different people.

The different types and aspects of a curriculum can also make it difficult to define – national, school, subject, actual and hidden are terms often used interchangeably, yet each has its own distinct meaning. In your work developing the curriculum, having a shared and well-understood definition of what the curriculum means to your school is crucial. Getting to grips with the following terms and definitions will help you establish your collective understanding.

DOI: 10.4324/9781003486589-3

Curriculum terms and definitions

A national curriculum

A national curriculum presents its nation's schools with guidance on what should be taught as part of their school curriculum. For most countries, this is done as a matter of social justice to ensure all children have equal access to a high-quality education.

However, while the intentions of a national curriculum are admirable, the practicalities of implementing one can often present substantial challenges for schools. For example, the amount of content and prescription in some national programmes can leave schools questioning how to fit it all into a busy timetable. In other cases, where national programmes lack detail, schools may need more clarity about what should be taught.

Ultimately, having a national curriculum can be a good thing to satisfy consistency and social justice issues, yet the best national curricula allow schools to make the necessary adaptations to meet their unique circumstances. In England, for example, most schools must plan their curriculum around the national curriculum. However, they also have the professional freedom to shape and adapt the requirements to create a more school-based offer.

A school curriculum

Unlike a national curriculum, a school curriculum is the unique programme of learning a school offers its children. Where there is a national curriculum to follow, teachers and senior leaders must skilfully amalgamate national requirements with more community-based needs and expertise. Getting the balance right here is crucial so that the curriculum does not become overcrowded or sway too far one way or the other. Figure 1.1 shows the various elements of a school curriculum.

Figure 1.1 Elements of a school curriculum.

A subject curriculum

Until recently, the term 'subject curriculum' was more commonly heard in secondary education, where subjects are taught separately. However, a subject-based approach to the curriculum is fast becoming popular in primary schools, mainly due to the emphasis on content sequencing, which is made easier by planning subjects discretely.

The term subject curriculum in primary schools is usually used to describe the progression and content of a singular subject, such as geography or history. Each subject curriculum should have its own progression map showing how the skills and knowledge of the subject progress over time.

While it is imperative for a school to map each subject's unique schema, in this book, the importance and practicalities of making meaningful links between subject disciplines remain a priority as a critical feature of effective primary education.

An early years curriculum

The term early years curriculum is typically used to refer to the curriculum for very young children, usually aged three to five years. In this book, no specific part of the development process is dedicated to the early years; however, as a curriculum leader, you must consider how your primary curriculum builds on what has already been learned in the earlier years. You can read more about the implications of this in Appendix 1.1.

Other curriculum types and terms

As well as the more common curriculum types already mentioned, there are also other terms you will need to be familiar with as you work through the curriculum development process. These refer to aspects of curricula rather than being standalone curriculum models. Here is a brief synopsis.

Intended curriculum

The intended curriculum refers to the curriculum you plan to teach. It includes the goals of your curriculum and the concepts, knowledge, skills and content you want your children to learn. A school's curriculum progression framework often sets out your intended curriculum.

Actual curriculum

The actual curriculum is what happens in the classroom and is the realisation of your intended curriculum. It is important not to assume that the actual curriculum (taught and experienced in the school) will always reflect the intended (planned for) curriculum. As most primary teachers will know, this is only sometimes the case. To ensure that your actual curriculum best reflects your intended curriculum teachers must plan carefully, and leaders must have a range of well-established monitoring activities to identify and address discrepancies between the two.

Learned curriculum

The learned curriculum is the concepts, knowledge, skills, and attitudes children learn from studying your curriculum. Sound assessment systems, which include low-stakes quizzes, questioning and more formal testing, should provide a clear picture of what children are learning.

Hidden curriculum

The hidden curriculum is a term often used to describe the incidental learning children do without teachers' explicit intent. This can include aspects of social and cultural learning, such as speaking to one another, following rules and displaying acceptable behaviour. For example, through interactions with their peers, teachers and other adults in school, children will learn important things such as how to treat people and play fairly with others. Therefore, the hidden curriculum is crucial for developing children as well-rounded, socially competent individuals. It is also a significant factor in the transference of cultural capital, which is addressed in Chapter 3.

  Task

Consolidating what the curriculum means to you and your school before beginning your curriculum development journey is essential. Use the following questions as a starting point for discussions with your colleagues and other stakeholders about how these terms and different types of curricula currently apply to your school. Remember, you can use or adapt the questions to meet your needs. Don't forget to record any valuable outcomes of your conversations for future reference.

- What is our shared understanding of the term 'school curriculum'?
- How do we currently plan our intended curriculum?
- How do we monitor and evaluate our actual curriculum?
- Are there discrepancies between our intended and actual curriculum? How do we know?
- What is the learned curriculum?
- How well do we balance national curriculum requirements with our school and community needs?
- What do we mean by the term 'hidden curriculum'?
- How do we ensure that children can learn the hidden 'stuff' of the curriculum?
- What are the main learning points from our discussions?

Summary

There are many different types of curricula and terms used to describe them. A school curriculum also has many additional aspects. Throughout this book, you will encounter many of these terms and be required to use them in your work with others. Therefore, all stakeholders must know the meaning of each term so that professional dialogue can begin from a place of shared understanding.

2

KNOWLEDGE AND THE CURRICULUM

A core purpose of any primary curriculum must be to help children acquire a breadth and depth of knowledge about the world. It is also critical for children to have purposeful and productive opportunities to use their knowledge.

This chapter explains why being explicit about the knowledge you teach in your curriculum is essential and identifies some of the most common types of knowledge. Moreover, it provides an excellent opportunity to reflect on the importance and place of knowledge in your current or new curriculum.

Why knowledge is important

Why is knowledge such a hot topic for the primary school curriculum? While research such as cognitive load[1] and cultural capital[2] theory has done much to raise the profile of knowledge in the curriculum, any primary

DOI: 10.4324/9781003486589-4

teacher knows that the crux of our work is to help children know and do more. If the children you teach have a broad knowledge base, it can help them solve problems, discuss and debate, reason and communicate. One of the most rewarding outcomes of a good knowledge base is seeing how it can stimulate children's curiosity, inspiring them to want to know more, develop their interests and, ultimately, their passions. Moreover, knowledge can help children make better-informed decisions – weighing up information, considering the pros and cons of a matter and making better life choices. There is also one other significant reason why we should aim to provide all children with a sound knowledge base: it is a matter of social justice, particularly for those children who do not have the opportunity to acquire such knowledge outside of school. For those children, often from more disadvantaged backgrounds, having a broad and diverse knowledge can help them better access a rich curriculum, especially when it comes to reading comprehension.[3]

Planning and choosing the knowledge for your curriculum can be a painstaking task and needs careful thought and consideration – something we will address later in this book. However, before you decide what knowledge to include, taking time to refresh or consolidate your understanding of the different types of knowledge can be a valuable exercise. With this in mind, the following paragraphs provide a brief overview of the different types of knowledge you'll need to consider for your curriculum. It is well worth sharing these with your colleagues so there is a shared understanding and vocabulary for developing knowledge in your curriculum.

Different types of knowledge

Substantive knowledge

Substantive knowledge, sometimes called declarative knowledge, is one of the knowledge types most familiar to primary schools. In her article 'Taking curriculum seriously', Christine Counsell describes substantive knowledge as 'the content that teachers teach as established fact.'[4] An example of substantive knowledge is knowing that the United Kingdom comprises multiple countries in one nation (England, Northern Ireland, Scotland, and Wales) or that the capital city of England is London.

Disciplinary knowledge

Disciplinary knowledge is much more nuanced than other types of knowledge. Because of this, the term is often misused, and the significance of disciplinary knowledge in the curriculum is sometimes overlooked. Counsell describes disciplinary knowledge as 'a curricular term for what pupils learn about how that knowledge was established, its degree of certainty and how it continues to be revised by scholars, artists or professional practice.'[4] In other words, each discipline has its own practices and methodologies which define how they are studied and knowledge gained. For example, in science, children learn that facts are established and refined through testing, observing and investigating, while in history, children learn how historical claims, arguments and accounts are constructed and proven by examining first and second-hand sources.

Procedural knowledge

Procedural knowledge is knowing how to do something or complete a specific task – in other words, knowing how rather than what. Procedural knowledge, for example, can be knowing how to use a thermometer to measure a liquid's temperature in science or how to use a tjanting to apply hot wax to a fabric to create a batik.

A good primary curriculum requires both substantive and procedural knowledge to be effective. For example, if children know what a batik and a tjanting are (substantive knowledge) and how to use a tjanting to apply hot wax (procedural knowledge), then this gives children the best chance of creating a successful batik.

Procedural and substantive knowledge must be planned in tandem to ensure both are taught and applied.

Core knowledge

Core knowledge is the non-negotiable facts (substantive knowledge), methodologies (disciplinary) and skills (procedural knowledge) your children need to learn to understand your curriculum's concepts and ideas. For many primary schools, especially those following a national curriculum, knowledge is often set out in programmes of study and is deemed statutory. However, this knowledge is often so broad that it does require some breaking down into smaller parts.

While you may be required to cover specific knowledge of a national curriculum, you must also carefully consider what local knowledge will form part of your core offering. For example, knowledge about local landmarks, historical buildings, or significant people will bring relevance and connectivity to nationally set programmes of study.

Hinterland knowledge

Counsell coined the phrase 'hinterland knowledge' in her 2018 blog, The Dignity of the Thing.[5] Counsell uses the term to describe the extra contextual knowledge children need to understand critical historical concepts or vocabulary. However, in this book, hinterland knowledge also applies to other subjects, as well as history.

Hinterland knowledge is a great way of adding interest, meaning and context to your curriculum's various topics and themes and can do much to engage children in their learning. For example, knowing that Guernica was painted in 1937 by Pablo Picasso is a substantive fact you might want children to know and remember as part of your art curriculum. However, knowing that the painting is blue, black and white, 11 feet tall and was painted as a reaction to the Nazi bombing of the Basque town of Guernica brings a rich and dynamic perspective to children's learning.

Sequencing knowledge

As important as the knowledge you choose for your curriculum is the sequence you present it in and the opportunities you provide for children to revisit it.

When sequencing substantive knowledge, you must ensure that fact A comes before fact B for fact B to be understood. This way, children can gradually develop their understanding of the concepts or themes of your curriculum logically.

Procedural knowledge also requires logical step-by-step sequencing. Children must master step A before they can perform step B. For example, children must know how to thread a needle before making a stitch. When they can make a simple single stitch, they can move on to running stitch. This is also important in mathematics, where small incremental skills can help children to solve more significant numerical problems.

Task

Take this opportunity to reflect on the place and effectiveness of knowledge in your current curriculum and how well it is taught, applied and sequenced. If you are looking to create a new curriculum, think about and discuss with others how knowledge will feature.

Summary

A curriculum with a broad and well-sequenced underpinning of knowledge can help all children build a robust understanding of the world. A great primary curriculum should also provide all children with engaging learning experiences. In other words, no primary curriculum should be a narrow menu of disparate and incoherent facts. It is crucial therefore, that your curriculum balances all types of knowledge to create optimum learning conditions for all children.

Ultimately, if you want your curriculum to be a powerful tool for social justice, it is not just the type of knowledge you teach but also about how many ways you support your children to use and apply it.

Notes

1   Sweller J. Cognitive load during problem solving: Effects on learning. *Cognitive Science.* 1988; 12: 257–85.
2   Bourdieu P. *Distinction: A Social Critique of the Judgement of Taste.* Routledge; 1987.
3   Hirsch Jr ED. Building knowledge: The case for bringing content into the language arts block and for a knowledge-rich curriculum core for all children. AFT – A union of Professionals – Building Knowledge. 2012.
4   Counsell C. Taking curriculum seriously. MyCollege. Published September 2018. Accessed 12 February 2024. https://my.chartered.college/impact_article/taking-curriculum-seriously/
5   Counsell C. Senior curriculum leadership 1: The indirect manifestation of knowledge: (A) curriculum as narrative. The dignity of the thing. Published April 2018. Accessed 12 February 2024. https://thedignityofthethingblog.wordpress.com/2018/04/07/senior-curriculum-leadership-1-the-indirect-manifestation-of-knowledge-a-curriculum-as-narrative/

References

Bourdieu P. *Distinction: A Social Critique of the Judgement of Taste.* Routledge; 1987.
Counsell C. Taking curriculum seriously. MyCollege. Published September 2018. Accessed 12 February 2024. https://my.chartered.college/impact_article/taking-curriculum-seriously/

Counsell C. Senior curriculum leadership 1: The indirect manifestation of knowl-
    edge: (A) curriculum as narrative. The dignity of the thing. Published April
    2018. Accessed 12 February 2024. https://thedignityofthethingblog.wordpress.
    com/2018/04/07/senior-curriculum-leadership-1-the-indirect-manifestation-of-
    knowledge-a-curriculum-as-narrative/
Hirsch Jr ED. Building knowledge: The case for bringing content into the language arts
    block and for a knowledge-rich curriculum core for all children. AFT – A union of
    Professionals – Building Knowledge. 2012.
Sweller J. Cognitive load during problem solving: Effects on learning. *Cognitive Science*.
    1988; 12: 257–85.

3

CULTURAL CAPITAL IN THE CURRICULUM

French sociologist Pierre Bourdieu first developed cultural capital theory in collaboration with Jean-Claude Passeron in the essay 'Cultural Reproduction and Social Reproduction',[1] to explain how power in society was transferred and social classes maintained. For Bourdieu, the more capital you have, the more powerful you are.

Since his book 'Distinction',[2] the phrase cultural capital has become much more commonplace in educational discourse, with the term finding its way into the English inspection system as the 'essential knowledge that children need to prepare them for their future success.'[3]

While cultural capital is an incredibly complex and nuanced social theory, there are many salient points to extrapolate concerning the curriculum. In this chapter, rather than focus on theory, which you can read more about in any of the books listed in Appendix 3.1, we'll focus on practical ways to support the development of all children's cultural capital through your curriculum.

DOI: 10.4324/9781003486589-5

An analogy

When explaining cultural capital to teachers, I usually use a simple analogy. You might like to use this with your staff – it always resonates. Imagine you have two children, Child A and Child B. Both children come to school with large pockets. In Child A's pockets is a breadth of cultural experiences, including theatre and gallery visits, a library full of stories and a rich vocabulary learned from high-quality conversations and interactions. Child A fits in with the school environment and does well. Child B's pockets are much less full. They also have some less positive experiences and behaviours, which makes fitting in with the social norms and expectations of the school more difficult. I'm sure you get the picture and recognise Child A and B. You've probably met them many times.

The Curriculum

As primary teachers, we interact with young children every day. We do this through our planned curriculum but also via the hidden curriculum. Through the hidden curriculum, we can help children understand socially acceptable norms and expectations, such as how to line up, share a book, play fairly, or resolve a conflict. You should always appreciate your crucial role as a teacher to make a difference through this type of interaction. Many schools also work hard to address academic disadvantage through initiatives, such as tutoring, mentoring and catch-up programmes, which can be helpful for children who need additional support.

However, while these things are crucial for addressing the disadvantages some children face, the curriculum can have a broader, more transformative impact on children's cultural capital. The following paragraphs provide helpful tips and tasks for improving your cultural offer.

Embed a range of cultural experiences

Sutton Trust asked parents how often they took their child to a cultural experience in the last six months (not including trips their children had taken with their school). It found that 'parents from higher social groups were more likely to have taken their children on cultural visits and to do so more often'.[4]

While this is perhaps no surprise, it does reinforce the importance of our role as educators in making these opportunities available to all children. For schools in more disadvantaged communities, embedding cultural experiences within the curriculum is vital, as statistically, these children are less likely to have those experiences with their families. While some cultural experiences, such as theatre trips and visits to national heritage sites, are expensive and therefore prohibitive for many schools, local alternatives often have a much-reduced cost or no cost at all. For example, taking children on a walk to a local place of worship, the local library, or a community art exhibition will enrich your curriculum and support the development of children's cultural capital. It is worth contacting such venues to see what cultural events they have planned that you can integrate into your curriculum.

Figure 3.1 provides ideas for places to visit within your locality to support children's cultural capital. There are ideas for various subjects, which

Figure 3.1 Places to visit to enhance children's cultural capital.

you can use as a starting point for discussions about cultural experiences in your curriculum.

 Task

Take the time, either on your own or with others, to reflect how many cultural experiences your school offers its children. Consider if they provide sufficient breadth and how equally they are distributed across the school.

Acknowledge children's existing cultural capital

Bourdieu acknowledged that, despite how it might sometimes seem, all children start their education with some cultural capital.

'When, for instance, the individual emerges onto the education market, he is already endowed with an inherited capital that, before any explicit education, can only be interpreted by the institution accepting him as being a gift.'[1]

When developing your curriculum, knowing and acknowledging the 'gifts' your children already have is imperative. Getting to know your children, their families, and your local community well will help you do this by developing a curriculum that builds on their unique experiences, traditions, beliefs and so on. Developing curriculum themes or topics around identity, family, traditions, and celebrations is a great way to include children's lived experiences and cultures in your curriculum.

Encourage parental involvement

Including parents, carers, and the wider community is crucial for a culturally rich and equitable curriculum. Encouraging parents to come into school and work with the children for activities, such as storytelling, baking and play in the early years can bring a more diverse dynamic to your curriculum and classroom. Not only can children enjoy valuable encounters with adults from different backgrounds, but they can also have the opportunity to observe different languages, habits and accents. If your community does not have a diverse demographic, it is still beneficial to invite parents and grandparents into school to share cultural and social expectations and build empathetic relationships. Moreover, the more parents understand what happens in school, the better they are placed to support children's learning at home – a crucial part of building children's cultural capital.

The best example I have ever seen of parental collaboration is in the Schools of Early Childhood in Reggio Emilia. Here, parents play a significant role in shaping and supporting the curriculum and are an invaluable part of the children's educational experience. Appendix 3.2 provides an overview of the Reggio Emilia Approach® and the importance of parental involvement in developing children's cultural capital.

Build a broad knowledge base

A broad knowledge base will help all children know more about the world's people, places and diverse cultures. It can also help them develop their opinions, perspectives, and viewpoints, which are essential for speaking articulately and confidently in various social contexts. Of course, having a good breadth and depth of knowledge is also a vital factor for academic success, for example, having the knowledge to pass exams, gain qualifications, secure a university place and so on.

So, as you look to develop or improve your curriculum, it is crucial to build a well-structured curriculum progression framework that sets out the knowledge you want your children to learn as they study your curriculum. You must ensure that the knowledge you do include builds incrementally over time and allows children to delve more deeply into any topics or issues they find interesting or even fascinating.

Finally, as children develop a broad knowledge base, it is important to consider how your pedagogic approach enables them to use and apply it. Debates, group discussions, investigations, creative processes, enquiries, and problem-solving activities are great ways to apply and reason with knowledge.

Value all subjects

Providing a broad and balanced curriculum, where all subjects are valued and well taught, is essential for developing primary children's cultural capital. It is also a typical feature of most primary schools. However, it is worth remembering that all children should have access to all curriculum areas, including the arts, sciences, humanities, and so on, no matter their starting point, abilities or needs. Narrowing the curriculum for all or some children will only create further gaps in children's cultural capital and exclude them from the opportunities and life chances they deserve.

Promote diversity

Ensuring your curriculum provides opportunities for all children to explore and appreciate diverse cultures is crucial to them becoming well-rounded and informed individuals. Introducing them to literature, music, art, faiths and traditions from around the world can develop, among other things, their appreciation, empathy and respect for others. Teaching children about the diverse histories and contributions of different cultures to the past and present will also help them to understand how all peoples have contributed to their everyday lives. If your school is part of a less diverse community, consider investing in high-quality resources that represent the art, music and literature from a diverse range of cultures to support your curriculum.

Encourage a rich vocabulary

A broad and rich vocabulary is a prerequisite for all children to articulate their knowledge and socialise confidently and appropriately with others. There are many ways to promote and extend children's vocabulary through your curriculum. One such way is to develop a comprehensive vocabulary framework to underpin your curriculum. This enables critical language for each subject discipline to be set out and then embedded into the lessons teachers teach and the resources they use to support children's learning. Teachers should use this vocabulary daily so it becomes a natural part of children's rich lexicon. Reading is, without a doubt, one of the best ways to improve all children's vocabulary, and it is crucial to embed plenty of rich reading opportunities throughout your curriculum. Classroom routines, such as story time, quiet reading and listening to readers are essential for developing a rich and ambitious vocabulary in all learners.

Remember the hidden curriculum

The daily interactions of the hidden curriculum help children develop the social values essential for building successful relationships with others. Learning about fairness, honesty, negotiation, cooperation and conflict resolution through peer-to-peer and adult-to-child interactions is fundamental to children's personal growth.

However, knowing that the hidden curriculum can unintentionally reinforce negative cultural assumptions and biases is also critical. For example, through their social groups, children may be exposed to racial or gender stereotyping that is unhelpful to their personal and social development. Therefore, it is important that adults in the school model the school's social and moral values, which are reinforced through assemblies, story times, playtimes and other 'hidden' learning opportunities.

Build a cultural offer

While most schools build cultural capital into the aims and aspirations of their curriculum, some decide to make this even more explicit by developing a cultural offer. A cultural offer identifies the planned cultural experiences that children will be entitled to as part of the broader curriculum. Having a cultural offer can help all stakeholders determine whether opportunities are equitable across the school. Appendix 3.3 provides an example of a cultural offer with a range of school, community, and expert-led activities.

   Task

Take a moment to reflect on your school's current cultural offer. How well do you help your children to acquire the cultural capital they need to succeed? Think about ways you might like to change or improve your offer. How do you think you could do this? Make notes to record your thoughts to refer to later in the process.

Summary

While, as primary practitioners, we can do much to help build children's cultural capital, it can take generations to develop and establish. As Bourdieu says, 'Cultural capital can only be transmitted at the cost of a considerable amount of time'.[1] Social injustices can be improved, but it is often a longer-term change rather than a short-term goal. This means it may take years to see any significant cultural shift.

As primary teachers, we know that even the smallest things can make a difference to the individual child. Talking to parents about home routines, listening to children talk about a special occasion, or simply sharing a beautiful book can all help improve a child's cultural capital.

However, no school can overcome all the disadvantages children may face beyond their school life, no matter how hard we try. Yet, providing support for parents, appropriate homework, lovely books to read, and suggestions of places to visit can address some of the cultural capital gaps in children's lives. In the quest to create equality for all, you, your school and your curriculum can be powerful agents of social change.

Notes

[1] Bourdieu P. *Cultural Reproduction and Social Reproduction. Knowledge, Education, and Cultural Change* (pp. 71–112). Routledge; 2018.
[2] Bourdieu, P. *Distinction: A Social Critique of the Judgement of Taste.* Routledge; 2010.
[3] Ofsted. Early years inspection handbook, Updated 19 January 2024. Accessed 12 February 2024. https://www.gov.uk/government/publications/early-years-inspection-handbook-eif/early-years-inspection-handbook-for-ofsted-registered-provision-for-september-2023#fn:15
[4] Montacute R, Cullinane C. How parents use financial and cultural resources to boost their children's chances of success. Parent Power 2018. Published September 2018. Accessed 12 February 2024. https://www. suttontrust.com/wp-content/uploads/2019/12/Parent-Power-2018.pdf

References

Bourdieu P. *Distinction: A Social Critique of the Judgement of Taste.* Routledge, 2010.
Bourdieu P. *Cultural Reproduction and Social Reproduction. Knowledge, Education, and Cultural Change* (pp. 71–112). Routledge; 2018.
Montacute R, Cullinane C. How parents use financial and cultural resources to boost their children's chances of success. Parent Power 2018. Published September 2018. Accessed 12 February 2024. https://www. suttontrust.com/wp-content/uploads/2019/12/Parent-Power-2018.pdf
Ofsted. Early years inspection handbook, Updated 19 January 2024. Accessed 12 February 2024. https://www.gov.uk/government/publications/early-years-inspection-handbook-eif/early-years-inspection-handbook-for-ofsted-registered-provision-for-september-2023#fn:15
Reggio Emilia Approach®. Accessed 12 February 2024. https://www.reggiochildren.it/en/reggio-emilia-approach

4

LOCALISING YOUR CURRICULUM

Curriculum localisation means making your school curriculum more relevant, meaningful, and effective in your local context. This is particularly important for those schools that structure their curriculum around national guidelines, as it can help children understand and appreciate the place they live and its interconnectedness with the rest of the world. Typical examples of curriculum localisation include local history studies, geographical fieldwork and the study of significant people and events in the locality.

This chapter provides ideas for integrating aspects of your locality into your curriculum, including helpful tools, materials and examples to inform your thinking. Use the information to reflect upon localisation in your existing curriculum or consider your aspirations for your new curriculum.

Aspects of localisation

The following points provide guidance on important aspects of curriculum localisation. Parental and family involvement in learning activities and

DOI: 10.4324/9781003486589-6

day to day routines of the school are also an excellent way to promote cultural relevance.

Keep things culturally relevant

Ensure your school curriculum reflects your community's traditions, cultures and values. You can do this through the themes and topics children study and through broader curriculum activities, such as school celebrations, extracurricular activities and within aspects of your 'hidden' curriculum.

Seek meaningful content

Integrate local content into the themes and topics you teach in your curriculum. For example, if children are learning about the history of the Second World War, look for ways to include stories, images, and historical evidence about how people in the locality were affected or made significant contributions. Using local archives, museums, and monuments is a good way for children to build their understanding of local historical issues.

Support flexibility

Encourage teachers to adapt their plans in light of the community's changing needs. For example, if the community demographic changes to include new cultures, families and traditions, you should adapt your curriculum to ensure representation and inclusion.

Link global issues

Provide opportunities for children to understand how local behaviours can impact the wider world. For example, by introducing class or school recycling practices, children can better appreciate how their actions can positively contribute to global issues such as waste management, pollution and climate change.

Gather feedback

Ensure there are opportunities for all stakeholders to contribute their thoughts and ideas to the effectiveness of your curriculum localisation.

Listening to stakeholders' views will help you to identify any necessary adjustments as your community and curriculum evolve.

Benefits of localisation

While we have already acknowledged the benefits of curriculum localisation for relevance and meaning, adding a local dimension to your curriculum has other advantages. One of the less talked about benefits of curriculum localisation is that it allows teachers to use active and engaging teaching strategies, such as investigation, enquiry, first-hand observation, and fieldwork. Moreover, getting children out and about and in the fresh air brings a new dynamic to your curriculum.

Local communities can benefit, too. As children learn about their local community, they tend to value it more. Knowing special places, monuments, natural resources, and local people can all help develop children's sense of pride in their surroundings. In addition, when children actively contribute to their locality through activities such as litter picking or bulb planting, they learn what it means to care for their community and its surroundings.

Finally, it is also important to point out that localising aspects of your curriculum can help save your school money. Travelling to places on foot or public transport rather than using expensive coach travel to go further afield is one of the great benefits of curriculum localisation.

Challenges of localisation

Despite the positive effects of localisation, there can be some drawbacks, particularly if the curriculum becomes over-localised. If we want children to become global citizens with a broad cultural capital, limiting children's learning by restricting their worldview would be counterintuitive. In other words, getting the balance right is critical.

Another significant challenge can be an increased workload for teachers. This is often due to the need to create resources that reflect the local context rather than being able to draw on quality commercial schemes.

  Task

Table 4.1 highlights some features of a well-balanced and localised curriculum. Read each feature and consider how well this reflects your current curriculum. Make notes about any ideas for future developments.

Table 4.1 Some features of a well-balanced localised curriculum

Feature	Evidence	Notes
Opportunities for local study are identified.	Teachers highlight opportunities for local study in each subject. In some cases, this reflects national curriculum requirements. For example, in the geography national curriculum in England, children are required to learn about the physical features of rivers. Studying a local river will allow children to develop and apply their knowledge of rivers using fieldwork skills. Such opportunities are set out in the schools' curriculum plans so that the local offer is visible across the whole school.	
Links between local and global aspects of the curriculum are well established.	Opportunities for children to make links between local, national and global contexts are well planned. Such activities allow children to observe similarities and differences between people, places and other vital matters such as ethical, moral or environmental issues. For example, children visit a local supermarket and learn about the different parts of the world their food comes from.	
Specialist learning weeks form part of the curriculum	Specialist weeks are integrated into the curriculum. For example, a whole school art week focuses on local landscapes and helps children learn drawing and painting techniques while reinforcing aspects of their geographical understanding. These are often planned and delivered with outside agencies offering curriculum expertise unavailable within the school.	
People from the community offer their expertise	Parents, carers, grandparents and other adults in the locality are invited to contribute to the curriculum. Businesspeople, residents, police community support officers, librarians and firefighters add valuable expertise to the curriculum. In disadvantaged communities where locals may be hesitant or lack the confidence to come into or contribute to school life, teachers give time to nurturing these relationships.	

Use these questions and your notes from Table 4.1 as a starting point for discussions with colleagues about localising your curriculum.

1. What is our current approach to curriculum localisation?
2. Is it well-planned or more ad hoc?
3. What resources do we have in the locality that could enhance our curriculum?
4. Do some subjects provide more local opportunities than others?
5. Are there any issues around adding more localised opportunities? How might we overcome these challenges?

Summary

Achieving the correct balance between local, national and global content in your curriculum is tricky but certainly possible. Local study is not something to be added on but a means of making your curriculum more meaningful and relevant for your children and should be an integral part of your curriculum planning.

However, while looking for and embedding local learning opportunities is good practice, it is essential not to over-localise your curriculum. Over-localising can create a lack of diversity and global perspective, which is not conducive to an ambitious curriculum or the development of global citizens.

5

PEDAGOGY MATTERS

Pedagogy is often confused with the curriculum itself; however, pedagogy and curriculum are two distinct entities. While the curriculum is what you teach, your pedagogy determines how you teach.

Most schools work hard to achieve a clear and consistent approach to teaching their curriculum. However, in some cases, the emphasis on what the curriculum covers takes priority over how it is taught.

In this chapter, you should reflect upon the pedagogical approach you already have in place in your school and consider what this means for the design or development of your curriculum. Moreover, if your pedagogy needs clarifying, updating or formalising, this chapter provides an excellent opportunity to consider how you might like to address this.

Why is pedagogy important?

Never underestimate the importance of your pedagogy. As a senior leader, I have seen poorly planned curricula taught well and brilliantly designed curricula taught poorly. Inevitably, great teaching always trumps even the

DOI: 10.4324/9781003486589-7

best-laid plans. For some teachers, especially those less experienced or less confident, having a clear and shared whole-school approach to teaching your curriculum can provide the tools and strategies they need to teach it well.

Of course, children will always benefit from the skills and mastery of a great teacher, but a consistent whole-school pedagogy can also offer many other advantages. For example, a consistent and coherent pedagogical approach means that as children move from one class or year group to another, they can better access new content as their means of doing so is already well established. That is, they do not need to adapt to or understand new approaches to teaching or learning as both are already familiar to them, even if the teacher or environment is different.

Teaching the whole child

While your pedagogy must help children learn the academic content of your curriculum, it must also support the whole child's development. Ensuring your pedagogy does this means including strategies such as play, investigation, problem-solving, group work and the opportunity for children to learn from practical and motivating experiences. Such teaching strategies will ultimately make your curriculum more engaging and more likely to support children's capacity to develop other skills, such as creative and critical thinking. Allowing such features to permeate your whole-school pedagogy is so important for primary children, especially if we want to ensure children feel listened to, trusted, and safe.

Choosing your pedagogy

The best pedagogical approaches amalgamate academic research with your school's educational beliefs. Some schools adopt a branded practice, such as Rosenshine principles[1] or the Reggio Emilia Approach®[2] and adapt it to fit their school. In contrast, some develop their own methods and approaches for reasons set out in the following paragraphs.

To create better cohesion with the school's curriculum vision

The approach a school takes to teaching the curriculum should reflect the intentions of their curriculum vision. For example, if developing children's speaking and listening skills is an aim for your curriculum, then teachers should include teaching strategies such as group discussion, debate, public speaking, peer-to-peer and group listening in their day-to-day classroom practice.

To meet the needs of the children

An effective pedagogy should meet the needs and characteristics of your children. This can include their cultural background, age, or academic abilities. For example, if a school has children with English as an additional language, then your pedagogy must include strategies which enable them to access your curriculum.

In response to change

Changes in technology, government, educational initiatives and research can significantly shape and influence a school's pedagogy. However, placing too much emphasis on shifting initiatives can adversely affect the stability and cause confusion for stakeholders and children.

To reflect community aspirations

Some schools involve the community, including parents, teachers and other stakeholders, in developing their pedagogy. This collaborative approach ensures that the values and aspirations of the broader community are reflected in the way the curriculum is taught. This can also bring greater support from the community. Reggio Emilia is a brilliant example of this.

Whether you decide to adapt a recognised pedagogical model or create your own, you should check that it provides the right amount of structure and guidance your teachers need to teach your curriculum well. Appendix 5.1 provides an overview of different pedagogical approaches and their defining features. It includes space for your own thoughts and ideas.

Pedagogy and curriculum development

Your pedagogy and your curriculum must work well together. For example, having a creative curriculum taught with an exclusively teacher-led approach would be counterintuitive. Finding harmony between your curriculum and your pedagogy is essential for the success of both.

Appreciating the nuances of your pedagogical approach and encouraging teachers to think carefully about the best methodology for any particular lesson is also essential. Moreover, it is also vital to ensure that your pedagogy has breadth. Using the same teaching methodologies in every lesson can become boring and cause some children to disengage.

Effective pedagogy is ultimately about having an agreed approach that meets your curriculum's needs and allows teachers to use their professional judgment to meet the needs of a lesson or children they teach.

  Task

The questions below will help you consider the best pedagogical approach for your school and what implications this might have for your curriculum. Remember to record your thoughts and ideas to refer to them later.

1. How do we believe children learn best?
2. What evidence or research do we have to prove this?
3. How does our pedagogical approach affect the design of our curriculum?
4. What teaching methodologies have we tried so far?
5. How might we adapt or improve these methodologies to better meet the needs of our children?

Making your pedagogy visible

Once you have decided upon your pedagogical approach, it is crucial to make it visible. This means that how you teach your curriculum is seen and not merely assumed. The Reggio Emilia Approach® has been doing this for decades and is a well-established practice. For example, children's learning is made explicit, visible, and evaluable through group work, open and shared documentation of learning, and constructive child–teacher talk. I have observed this in practice, and it is the best example I have ever seen of a clear and visible pedagogy shared across multiple schools and settings.

You can make your pedagogy visible in many ways. But how you do this will depend on your approach and what you want to demonstrate.

For example, if your pedagogy promotes investigation as a teaching strategy, you might display photographs of children showing this way of working in different subjects and activities. Or, if group working is an important feature, teachers should have the flexibility to change and adapt the children's learning spaces to accommodate group work and discussion.

It is also helpful to build the language of learning into everyday routines and activities. Hence, children become familiar with any terms relating to your approach and can use them when discussing their learning. For example, if observation is a key feature of your pedagogical approach, children should be taught vocabulary such as inspect, monitor, scrutinise, study, examine and watch.

It is essential to share your pedagogy with parents and other stakeholders. Again, there are many ways to do this, but it is worth putting a pedagogical statement on your school website or in other shared documentation, such as your school prospectus.

Summary

Not all pedagogy is the same; what works for one school may not work for another. You and your colleagues must decide what works best for you and your children and draw upon quality research and your collective knowledge to create an effective approach. Moreover, finding a synchronicity between your curriculum and how it is taught is crucial for how well children learn.

Whatever pedagogical approach you take, regularly reviewing and reflecting upon its effectiveness, as with your curriculum, is vital. As times and situations change and cohorts of children move on, you may need to make adaptations to better suit your children's learning needs.

Notes

[1]   Rosenshine B. Principles of instruction research-based strategies that all teachers should know. American Educator. Published online 2012. Accessed 12 February 2024. https://www.aft.org/sites/default/files/Rosenshine.pdf

[2]   Reggio Children. Reggio Emilia Approach. Accessed 12 February 2024. https://www.reggiochildren.it/en/reggio-emilia-approach/

References

Reggio Children. Reggio Emilia Approach. Accessed 12 February 2024. https://www. reggiochildren.it/en/reggio-emilia-approach/

Rosenshine B. Principles of instruction research-based strategies that all teachers should know. American Educator. Published online 2012. Accessed 12 February 2022. https://www.aft.org/sites/default/files/Rosenshine.pdf

6

THE IMPORTANCE OF GOOD SUBJECT LEADERSHIP

Having been a subject leader in many different schools for various curriculum subjects, I can honestly say it's a tough job. Yet, designing, leading and managing a great curriculum is only possible for any school when subject leaders are well-informed, knowledgeable and resilient.

In most primary schools, subject leaders take responsibility for leading one curriculum subject. However, in some schools, especially small ones, staff often lead multiple subjects. This can make subject leadership an even greater challenge.

So, while we know that school improvement ultimately remains the responsibility of the headteacher and governing body, the role of the subject leader is vital for the effective teaching and learning of subjects. Therefore, this chapter explores the roles and responsibilities of subject leaders and offers some food for thought for the importance of subject leaders in your curriculum development.

DOI: 10.4324/9781003486589-8

Strategic direction

First and foremost, subject leaders must know the strengths and weaknesses of the subject they lead. Once your subject leaders have this information, they can identify areas for strategic improvement and begin making plans to address them.

In some schools, subject leaders create individual subject development plans. Ideally, these form part of a larger whole-school curriculum development plan. An example subject plan for geography is provided in Appendix 6.1.

   Task

Use these questions as a starting point for discussions with your subject leaders about the strategic direction of their subject.

1. What are the aims for [subject]?
2. Why are these aims important?
3. Is there a development plan for [subject]?
4. What aspects of [subject] need improvement?
5. Do the subject's aims align with school, national and statutory requirements?
6. Do the subject's aims align with our school's curriculum vision?

Curriculum design

Subject leaders play a significant role in helping you design your curriculum. This includes working together to identify the big ideas of your curriculum, providing guidance and making decisions about the disciplinary concepts of their subject, selecting and sequencing subject knowledge to build a cohesive and well-sequenced curriculum progression framework, working with other subject leaders to identify links and connections with other subjects, ensuring any national requirements are covered and supporting teachers with lesson plans and resources.

Teaching, learning and assessment

Subject leaders are also critical to the successful implementation of your curriculum. Their role includes ensuring teachers are up to date with curriculum content and teaching strategies and have the right resources to teach the subject well. To do this, subject leaders must keep abreast of any new subject research or initiatives and be ready to disseminate this information to staff.

It is also crucial that subject leaders ensure meaningful assessment procedures are in place to enable teachers to make sound judgements about what children know and can do. Analysis of teachers' assessments will inform subject leaders how well children learn the subject they lead and enable them to identify gaps and misconceptions. Knowing where gaps and misconceptions exist will help the subject leader to adapt the curriculum or introduce teaching strategies to address them.

   Task

The following questions will help subject leaders to reflect on the effectiveness of teaching, learning and assessment of their subject.

1. How do you ensure [subject] knowledge is learned and retained?
2. How do you ensure that pupils with SEND can access [subject]?
3. Are expectations high enough?
4. How are misconceptions addressed in [subject]? Can you give an example?
5. How can you avoid unnecessary workload for teachers in [subject]?
6. What [subject] resources do you offer children, and how are they matched to your curriculum?
7. What do children learn well in [subject]?
8. What do children need to study in greater depth?
9. What does challenge look like in [subject]?
10. What are the enrichment opportunities in [subject]?
11. How did you plan your curriculum to ensure there is progression?
12. Can you pick a concept from [subject] and explain its progression from the early years to Year 6?

Monitoring and evaluating

A crucial part of any subject leader's work is to ensure that adequate systems are put in place to monitor and evaluate the impact of your curriculum. Being able to answer questions, such as 'Is the planned content in the curriculum well taught?' and 'Does it help children to learn and make good progress?' is an essential part of subject leadership and is crucial for effective evaluation of progress. Moreover, monitoring the curriculum will help your subject leaders identify future developments.

Activities such as lesson observations, work sampling, talking to staff and children, and data analysis are all helpful ways of discovering what is happening in the classroom. However, there must be senior-level support for such activities, especially if the subject leader is not an expert in the subject they lead.

The size of your school may also be a significant factor in how easily and effectively subject leaders conduct monitoring activities. There are pros and cons for both large and small schools. For example, in larger schools, monitoring activities can become very time-consuming due to the number of classes. Monitoring can be challenging in smaller schools, too. This is usually because subject leaders are responsible for multiple subjects. Where teachers lead multiple subjects, the time necessary to monitor them can result in significant time away from their classes.

Due to the sensitive nature of some of this work, subject leaders should conduct their monitoring activities mindfully. Any monitoring activity should aim to identify areas of strength and improvement, and it is imperative that all stakeholders feel on board with this shared purpose. Being positive, sensitive and tactful with feedback is part of creating a positive culture of monitoring and evaluation.

Leading and supporting

Subject leaders should provide staff with the support they need to teach and understand the unique characteristics of each subject. When teachers know and understand a subject well, children's learning is much more likely to be effective.

Subject leaders can help teachers achieve better subject knowledge in many ways. Professional development opportunities can include formally planned activities, such as subject training days and one-to-one coaching. Alternatively, more ad hoc opportunities, such as answering a quick question over lunch, can be helpful.

Most importantly, your subject leaders must advocate for the subject they lead as, leading by example is a powerful motivator for improvement. Modelling effective teaching methods, displaying good examples of children's work and celebrating success stories are all part of being a great subject leader.

   Task

Subject leaders can use the following questions to consider the support they offer others.

1.   How does a new staff member know what happens in [subject]?
2.   How do I support staff, both formally and informally?
3.   What professional development opportunities have I provided for staff?
4.   What are the critical areas for professional development?
5.   How do I lead others in my subject?

Subject expertise and keeping up-to-date

Having subject expertise and up-to-date knowledge of subject research is crucial for subject leaders. The demand for an ambitious curriculum means all leaders must be on their A-game when leading their subject.

It is vital that leaders frequent subject-specialist websites for new research or issues around subject inspections and reports. It is also advantageous for subject leaders to join academic associations that can offer them subject expertise and support. The Historical Association[1] and Geographical Association[2] are examples, but there are many others that relate to numerous curriculum areas.

It is also important for your subject leaders to be aware that the knowledge and understanding required for subjects will change over time – for example, new historical discoveries or scientific findings. Therefore, they must endeavour to stay updated with developments in their subject area to be fully effective.

Finally, ask your subject leaders to look for and attend networking opportunities. These can be in person or virtual. Such events are perfect for leaders to share their experiences and seek the knowledge and expertise of others.

   Task

Subject leaders can use the following questions to consider how well they develop their expertise and keep current in their subject.

1. How do I keep up to date with current issues for [subject]?
2. How am I developing my [subject] expertise?
3. What support do I need to help me lead [subject] more effectively?

Leading maths and English

Subject leaders for maths and English often have a slightly different challenge than other subject leaders. This is because free national or published schemes are used in most English-speaking primary schools as a basis for these subjects. Such schemes are popular because of the large amount of curriculum content that needs to be taught in both maths and English and the level of expertise that subject leaders would need to create bespoke school-based schemes.

However, even with a scheme in place, leading the subjects of maths and English presents many other unique challenges. For example, the fact that these subjects are often formally tested means that subject leaders are under significant pressure to track and monitor children's progress and to raise levels of children's achievements year after year. Moreover, these subjects often come under greater external scrutiny, adding a more stressful dimension to the role.

While these subjects are not explicitly addressed in this book, the processes described can still apply meaningfully to maths and English. Even if you have maths or English schemes in place, it is worth using the process to review their effectiveness and see where they can be integrated within other subjects of your curriculum.

Subject leadership and inspection

Many countries have some form of external accountability process for inspecting the quality of education schools provide. These external evaluations are a time when subject leaders will naturally feel the pressure of subject leadership. Being well prepared for such events by being knowledgeable about the things highlighted in this chapter will help your subject leaders feel well-prepared.

Success in such external inspections depends heavily on subject leaders knowing their subject well and its impact on children's learning. Engaging knowledgeably in conversations and interrogations about their subject is crucial, as is being clear about what they want children to learn as part of the curriculum.

Summary

Subject leaders are crucial for a well-organised, rich and ambitious curriculum. Great subject leaders contribute not only to subject expertise but also provide effective support for others.

Subject leaders should be fully supported by senior leaders in the school. When support systems are in place subject leaders feel more empowered and confident to lead and challenge existing practices. Of course, this is never truer than if a subject leader is newly appointed, a non-specialist or facing the ordeal of an impending inspection.

Notes

[1]   History Association. Primary. Accessed 12 February 2024. https://www.history.org.uk/

[2]   Geographical Association. Curriculum support. Accessed 12 February 2024. https://geography.org.uk/curriculum-support/geography-subject-leadership-in-primary-and-secondary-schools/

References

Geographical Association. Geography subject leadership. Accessed 12 February 2024. https://geography.org.uk/curriculum-support/geography-subject-leadership-in-primary-and-secondary-schools/

Historical Association. Primary. Accessed 12 February 2024. https://www.history.org.uk/

7

THE COMPONENT PARTS OF A ROBUST CURRICULUM

Although every school's curriculum is unique, there are six key components that will help any school to build its best curriculum. These are, big ideas, subject concepts, a progression framework, curriculum narratives, resources and sound assessment procedures. These components build on one another to provide a coherent structure for schools to add their own content, pedagogy, aims and outcomes.

This chapter will explain each critical component and provide examples to help you understand them. You do not have to begin building these key components yet as that is addressed in Phase 3 of this book.

Big ideas

Big ideas are significant concepts that set out the academic aspirations for your curriculum and provide a means of prioritising and organising the subject concepts, knowledge and skills of your curriculum progression framework. Examples of big ideas include concepts such as investigation,

DOI: 10.4324/9781003486589-9

creativity, processes, communication and environment. Significantly, big ideas transcend multiple subjects and provide an excellent way to achieve coherence across the whole curriculum.

Appendix 7.1 provides a more detailed look at the role and importance of big ideas in your curriculum.

 Task

Read Appendix 7.1, then reflect on the place of big ideas in your existing curriculum or how they may feature in your new curriculum. You can use the questions below as a starting point for your thinking.

1. Does our current curriculum have clearly defined big ideas?
2. Do our big ideas help us to organise and prioritise the concepts, knowledge and skills of our curriculum?
3. Do we want big ideas for our curriculum?

If you want to establish big ideas for your curriculum, then Chapter 10, in Phase 3 will guide you through a series of practical activities to do so.

Subject concepts

Subject concepts are the central ideas of a subject – for example, habitats in science or colour theory in art and design. Unlike big ideas, subject concepts are smaller, more specific and not usually transferable across subjects. However, this rule has some exceptions; for example, the concept of weather can apply to geography or science. You can read more about subject concepts in Appendix 7.2.

 Task

Read Appendix 7.2, then use the questions below as a starting point for discussions with colleagues about how subject concepts might feature in your curriculum.

1. Does our current curriculum have clearly defined subject concepts?
2. Do the subject concepts in our curriculum help us identify the knowledge and skills that need to be taught?
3. How could we develop the use of subject concepts in our developing or new curriculum?

Curriculum progression framework

Your curriculum progression framework will help you organise the core knowledge (substantive, disciplinary and procedural) children need to learn to understand your curriculum's big ideas and concepts. Your progression framework should be well sequenced so that children can progress from point A to point B towards the endpoints or goals of your curriculum. It should also highlight opportunities for children to revisit and consolidate prior knowledge and skills. Appendix 7.3 provides more detail about this component of your curriculum.

 Task

Read Appendix 7.3, then reflect upon the effectiveness of your current curriculum progression framework, using the questions below as a starting point.

1. Is our current curriculum built on a cohesive progression framework?
2. Are the knowledge and skills set out sequentially?
3. Does our progression framework help children understand our curriculum's big ideas?
4. How might we want or need to adapt our current progression framework to be more effective?

Curriculum narratives

Your curriculum, just like the plot of a film or book, is a story told over time – it begins by laying the foundations and setting the scene, unfolds into a deep and engaging narrative and ends by tying all the loose ends together to provide a satisfying conclusion. Along the way, there may be twists and turns, flashbacks and meaningful connections between subjects and content and, like any good story, your curriculum should be engaging, irresistible, and unforgettable.

In most primary schools, each subject has its own narrative, told through a series of topics or projects and the lessons within them. Topics and projects from each subject then come together to build your whole curriculum narrative.

Appendix 7.4 provides more detail about curriculum narratives.

Task

Read Appendix 7.4, then use the questions below following questions to consider the place of narratives in your curriculum.

1. Are there currently clear narratives for the subjects of our curriculum?
2. Do our topics or projects help tell a cohesive story from the beginning to the end of our curriculum?
3. Are there any obvious gaps in the [subject] narrative?
4. How well do our subject narratives interconnect with other subjects?
5. Does our curriculum have a cohesive narrative overall?
6. How might we develop or improve the narrative of [subject]?
7. How might we develop or improve the narrative of our curriculum overall?

In Chapter 13, you'll have the opportunity to create your curriculum narratives.

Curriculum resources

Resources are often a forgotten part of the curriculum development process. In the past, many teachers have looked online for free or mass-produced resources; however, this practice is changing, with many schools realising that bespoke resources are ultimately better for helping teachers teach what is planned in their intended curriculum.

You can read more about the importance of curriculum resources in Appendix 7.5.

    Task

Read Appendix 7.5, then look at the questions below to consider how you might like to develop your approach to resourcing your curriculum.

1. How do we currently resource our curriculum?
2. Are our current resources of a high standard?
3. How well do our resources support children's learning?
4. What changes could we make to improve the quality of resources for our curriculum?

Chapter 14 provides a step-by-step process for creating knowledge organisers as a starting point for resourcing your curriculum.

Assessment

The assessment materials and processes you use to assess children's learning should be integral to your curriculum. Insightful assessment means that teachers have the information they need to understand what children know and can do and to inform their future planning. For curriculum or subject leaders, assessment is vital for understanding the overall impact of your curriculum and having the knowledge you need to make any necessary changes.

Any assessment materials and systems should align with your intended curriculum. This is sometimes hard if you use an off-the-shelf assessment package, and if you decide to do this, you will need to ensure that your curriculum content is well-matched.

You can read more about effective assessment practices in Appendix 7.6.

Task

Read Appendix 7.6, then use the questions below to reflect further.

1. How do we currently assess children's learning?
2. Does our current assessment practices help us to identify gaps in our curriculum?
3. Are our assessment systems or practices well matched to our intended curriculum?
4. What could we do to improve our assessment practices?

In Chapter 15, you can create low-stakes quizzes to help you assess your children's understanding of your curriculum.

Summary

This chapter, along with the appendices provided, should have given you plenty of food for thought about the crucial parts of a robust curriculum and the curriculum you would like to create. It should also have helped you to reflect on the curriculum you currently have in place and how it might need to be refined, adapted or improved. When all these critical parts are in place, the curriculum structure will look like the model shown in Appendix 7.7. In Chapter 8, you can use your thoughts and ideas from the tasks in this chapter to help you create a vision statement and development plan for your curriculum.

PHASE 1: CHECKLIST

THE KNOWLEDGE-BUILDING PHASE

You have reached the end of the first phase of this book. You will have begun to build a picture of your school's strengths and needs and know if you need to create a new curriculum or improve your existing one. Use this checklist to help you reflect on your work in this phase.

During this phase, you will have:

- ✓ Familiarised yourself and other stakeholders with the curriculum development process using the Curriculum Development Wheel.
- ✓ Discussed what the curriculum means to you and your school and agreed on a shared vocabulary.
- ✓ Considered the importance of different types of knowledge and thought about how to best use it in your new or existing curriculum.
- ✓ Reflected on the importance of cultural capital and thought about ways to improve or include a cultural offer as part of your curriculum.
- ✓ Considered how you might want to localise aspects of your curriculum and begun to think about some of your locality's human and physical resources.

DOI: 10.4324/9781003486589-10

✓ Discussed and agreed which pedagogical approach or style you want to use to teach your curriculum.

✓ Clarified the role of subject leaders in developing your curriculum and used the tasks to gather feedback from your subject leaders about the subjects they lead.

✓ Learned about the different parts of a robust curriculum and how these link to form a cohesive structure.

PHASE 2: SYNOPSIS

THE GOAL-SETTING PHASE

In this second phase of the book, the goal-setting phase, you can use your accumulated knowledge to decide your way forward – either by creating a new curriculum or by setting goals to refresh your existing curriculum. This phase lets you visualise these goals and create a practical plan to achieve them.

As in previous chapters, there are a range of practical tasks for you to carry out, either individually or with colleagues and a variety of useful templates, activities and examples. As always, it is up to you whether you use these, but in either case, I'm sure they will help guide your thinking.

By the end of this phase, you will have a clear vision for your curriculum and a logical, planned means of achieving it. It will likely take one month to complete, as you have already done much of the groundwork, in the first phase. However, don't worry if it takes you longer. This phase is essential for knowing what you want and how you are going to achieve it.

DOI: 10.4324/9781003486589-11

8

CREATING YOUR CURRICULUM VISION

Throughout the first phase of this book, you will have developed a better understanding of your current curriculum and should now have a good idea about what you want for your new or improved curriculum.

In this chapter, you can consolidate your ideas to build a vision for your new or improved curriculum by establishing its overarching aims and purpose. By the end of the chapter, you'll have a clear and inspiring curriculum vision statement and a practical strategic plan for developing, designing and implementing your curriculum.

What is a curriculum vision statement?

Your curriculum vision statement is a document that sets out the broad aims and purpose of your curriculum and establishes the guiding principles that shape its design and implementation. It outlines your overarching curriculum philosophy and determines the pedagogical approach that underpins it.

DOI: 10.4324/9781003486589-12

In his book *Principled Curriculum Design*, Professor Dylan Wiliam suggests seven fundamental principles of curriculum design.[1]

These are:

- balance
- rigorous
- coherent
- vertically integrated
- appropriate
- focused
- relevant

Some schools use these principles verbatim to develop their curriculum vision, while others prefer to create something more bespoke. You can choose to do either, but remember, this is your curriculum; therefore, you should be entirely convinced, comfortable and confident that your vision statement truly reflects the unique characteristics of your curriculum.

Starting point

So, how can you begin to create an authentic statement that reflects your unique curriculum? Firstly, it is essential to recognise that creating your curriculum vision should involve all stakeholders. This is crucial for buy-in, understanding and commitment, ultimately giving you a better chance of achieving your goals.

It is also important to reflect upon the notes you have made throughout the first phase of the book. Ask yourself, 'What are the strengths of our school curriculum?' and 'What are our hopes and ambitions?' Map out these ideas, as they will begin to form the basis of a vision for your curriculum going forward.

Use the task questions to discuss your ideas with your colleagues.

 Task

Discussing the vision for your curriculum with others is the best way to start this process. The following questions provide a good starting point for this. Best practice would suggest you use the questions with different groups – teachers, parents, governors, and so on – to gather a good range of perspectives. It's helpful to record their responses as these will provide a reference point for you as you develop your vision statement.

1.   What are the main goals and ambitions of our curriculum?
2.   What are our non-negotiable principles?
3.   What do we want people to say about our curriculum?
4.   What community and cultural values should influence our curriculum?
5.   What is unique about us?
6.   What style of curriculum do we want?
7.   How do we want to teach our curriculum?
8.   What does a good education mean to our school?

Consolidate

Once you have collated responses to your questions, you will begin to see a vision for your curriculum emerging. Nevertheless, if you want to consolidate things further, Appendix 8.1 provides the guidance and resources you need to do so practically and encourages collaborative working amongst stakeholders.

Next steps

Once you have gathered all the necessary information, you'll be ready to make a first draft of your curriculum vision. At this stage, it does not need to be the finished article but simply a document you can refer to when making decisions about the design and development of your curriculum. Appendix 8.2 provides a polished example, but don't expect yours to be so defined at this stage. Take your time getting to this point; eventually, you can firm yours up into a similar document, but for now, a rough draft is good enough.

Summary

Your curriculum vision statement is crucial for communicating the intentions and ambitions of your curriculum within the school to those deeply involved in its development and externally to outside agencies, including parents. Working collaboratively with others to create your vision is paramount for ensuring it reflects your school community. You can now use your drafted vision statement to help you build your curriculum development plan.

Note

[1] Wiliam D. Principled Curriculum Design. SSAT (The Schools Network) Ltd. Published October 2013. Accessed June 2023. https://webcontent.ssatuk.co.uk/wp-content/uploads/2013/09/Dylan-Wiliam-Principled-curriculum-design-chapter-1.pdf

Reference

Wiliam D. Principled Curriculum Design. SSAT (The Schools Network) Ltd. Published October 2013. Accessed 12 February 2024. https://webcontent.ssatuk.co.uk/wp-content/uploads/2013/09/Dylan-Wiliam-Principled-curriculum-design-chapter-1.pdf

9

CREATING YOUR CURRICULUM DEVELOPMENT PLAN

Your curriculum development plan is a document that translates your curriculum vision into a series of practical activities that will help you achieve your curriculum goals. It should include your priorities, development activities, and logistical considerations, such as costs and timelines. The priorities in your development plan should connect to your curriculum vision statement. For example, if one of your principles is to provide a knowledge-rich curriculum (and through your knowledge gathering work you know this needs improving) then a priority may be to, 'Improve the body of knowledge taught in the curriculum'.

This chapter provides you with guidance for creating your curriculum development plan.

Less is more

As you build your curriculum development plan, consider it a working document. There is no point in making highly detailed plans months, if not years, before you action them. As you work through the curriculum

DOI: 10.4324/9781003486589-13

development process, you will likely want to make tweaks and adaptations to your original plans due to the learning experiences you encounter along the way. Your plan will give you the steer you need to stay focused on what matters and not become distracted by more peripheral activities.

Your curriculum development plan is also helpful in explaining your intentions to other stakeholders, including external agencies, such as an inspection body. For example, if an area of your curriculum still requires improvement at the time of your school inspection, then showing that it is part of your development plan is vital for demonstrating your understanding of your curriculum's needs.

Formatting your curriculum development plan

A curriculum development plan can take many different forms, how you do yours depends on your school's preferred means of documentation. Typically, development plans are produced using word processing or spreadsheet software. Component-wise, plans often include the following headings:

- Priorities
- Development activities
- Start date
- End date
- Cost
- Success criteria
- Monitoring activities

Building your plan

The following paragraphs set out guidance for completing each section of your curriculum development plan. It will be helpful for you to have your curriculum vision statement at hand to ensure your plan directly delivers on your statement.

Remember, as with everything else in this book, the following points are only guidance, so don't worry if you decide to do yours differently. There is no one way of doing this.

Appendix 9.1 provides a template for a typical curriculum development plan.

Establish your priorities

A handful of well-written, strategic priorities will make it easier for all stakeholders to understand what matters most about the development of your curriculum. Your priorities should be concise, avoid jargon and be relevant to your curriculum vision. As you write your priorities, it is helpful to begin them with an active verb, such as improve, develop, expand, create, explore, establish, etc.

 Task

Begin drafting your curriculum priorities. Keep them brief and focused so all stakeholders can easily understand them. You must write them in sequence, so think carefully about how one priority might lead to another. Remember, your priorities should reflect the areas of your curriculum you want to develop or improve and link to your curriculum vision statement.

Describe your development activities

Once you have established your priorities, you should describe what you will do to achieve them. A simple sentence or two will suffice but remember to sequence them appropriately so that each activity builds on the previous. If the priority requires multiple activities, break them down accordingly so they are manageable. Table 9.1 shows a curriculum priority alongside its corresponding development activities.

Table 9.1 Example of curriculum priority with development activities

Priority	Development activities
Improve the body of knowledge in the curriculum.	• Review core knowledge in [subject/s]. • Address knowledge gaps in [subject/s]. • Check and improve progression of knowledge in all subjects. • Check connectivity and coherence of knowledge across the curriculum progression framework. • Identify core knowledge in lesson planning. • Improve body of knowledge in teaching resources.

Task

Draft the development activities that will help you achieve your curriculum priorities. It is acceptable to keep them brief at this stage; you can always add further details and amendments as you work through them. You can also add more activities as you progress, breaking them down into smaller chunks or adding more activities as needed.

Set your timescales

As part of your plan, it is important to establish your timescales and deadlines, as this will help you to consider how long the whole process will take. It will also make you think hard about the scope of the work. It is often surprising how long the curriculum development process can take, and you should be realistic about the time needed to avoid putting undue pressure on yourself and your colleagues.

Once established, you should do your best to stick to your schedule to avoid work piling up, but don't worry if you must delay, postpone or revisit things. It is normal to go back and forth with activities. That is perfectly acceptable as long as you can communicate why you have not made your intended progress.

Task

Add your proposed timescales and deadlines to your curriculum development plan. Discuss them with your senior leaders and other colleagues — are they achievable?

Acknowledge your budgetary needs

One of the most forgotten aspects of curriculum development is the associated costs — for example, covering non-contact time for yourself and subject leaders or the purchase of teaching resources. These costs can add up significantly over time and should be considered and allocated fairly. Although unexpected expenses will inevitably arise, it is essential to plan as best you can in line with the school's budget.

Task

Discuss the prospective costs of developing your curriculum with your senior leaders and governors, and then add them to your curriculum development plan.

Identify your success criteria

Success criteria are a vital part of your curriculum development plan as they provide a benchmark against which you can measure the success of your actions. Again, simple statements are enough – remember, you can always add more detail as your work develops. It is also important to seek input from the relevant stakeholders to agree what success looks like for each priority. Table 9.2 provides an example of success criteria.

Task

Look at each priority on your curriculum development plan and write a simple statement to define your success criteria. Ask yourself, 'What would be the ideal outcome for this priority?' Keep your statements simple to avoid confusion or misinterpretation by others.

Consider your monitoring opportunities

Although you will not yet have begun to put your curriculum development activities into action, it is worth considering how you might eventually

Table 9.2 Example of curriculum priority with success criteria

Priority	Success criteria
Improve the body of knowledge in the curriculum.	Core knowledge is identified for all curriculum subjects. Core knowledge is well-sequenced and set out clearly in the curriculum progression framework. Teachers identify core knowledge for each lesson. Teaching and learning resources reflect the core knowledge of the lesson. Children demonstrate an improved body of knowledge.

want to monitor them. We will look at this in more detail in Phase 4 of this book, but for now, some brief suggestions will be helpful. There are different types of monitoring activities you can suggest, anything from work sampling to opportunities for professional dialogue and talking to the children. Still, you can be flexible with your ideas at this stage.

Task

Add the relevant monitoring activities against each of your priorities. You might also want to identify who will carry out each monitoring activity – it doesn't always have to be you – teachers, subject leaders, senior leaders and governors should also take part in evaluating the progress and impact of your curriculum development plan.

Summary

Your curriculum development plan will help you achieve the goals and ambitions of your curriculum vision – a flexible working document that helps steer your development work and keeps everyone on track.

How you format your plan is optional, but it is worth sticking to the suggested headings for simplicity and to prevent unnecessary workload. Keep statements jargon-free so that all stakeholders can understand your curriculum priorities and see how they connect to the vision for your curriculum.

Phase 3 will now help you develop the priorities set out in your curriculum development plan. You can choose the appropriate chapters to meet your specific needs.

PHASE 2: CHECKLIST

THE GOAL-SETTING PHASE

You have reached the end of the second phase. During this phase, you will have agreed on a vision for your curriculum and created a curriculum development plan to determine how you will achieve it. Use this checklist to help you reflect on your work in this phase.

During this phase, you will have:

- ✓ Worked with all stakeholders to create a unique vision for your school curriculum.
- ✓ Drafted a short curriculum vision statement.
- ✓ Used your curriculum vision statement to help you draft a curriculum development plan.
- ✓ Discussed and shared your curriculum development plan with all stakeholders so everyone knows their role.

DOI: 10.4324/9781003486589-14

PHASE 3: SYNOPSIS

THE DESIGN AND CREATE PHASE

In this third and most creative phase of the book, you'll begin to either design and build a new curriculum or update and refresh aspects of your current curriculum.

Your curriculum development plan will tell you which aspects to work on, and you can choose the chapters you feel best meet your development needs. For example, if you need to clarify or create big ideas for your curriculum, you should begin at Chapter 10. If you want to improve the knowledge and sequencing of your curriculum, then go straight to Chapter 11. If you plan to build an entirely new curriculum, start at the beginning of Phase 3 and work through each of the interconnecting chapters.

As with all other phases, there are numerous tasks to help you address various issues of your curriculum development plan. If the activities provided are not exactly what you need, you can adapt them or use them as inspiration for creating activities that are precisely right for you.

DOI: 10.4324/9781003486589-15

This phase may take some time to complete – up to 18 months or longer, depending on what you need to do and your starting point. Don't worry about this – it is to be expected. I have known this part of the process takes several years to get right, and it must be right, so there is no point in rushing. It is much better to take the time to refine, test, edit and perfect.

10

ESTABLISHING YOUR BIG IDEAS

If you want to establish big ideas for your curriculum, this chapter will help you do that. As already explained in Chapter 7, your big ideas are significant concepts that provide the academic intent for your curriculum. They will also help you to translate your curriculum vision into an educational reality.

This chapter, like others, provides a series of simple, practical tasks to help you establish the big ideas of your curriculum. You can carry out these tasks with teaching staff and other stakeholders to share ideas and expertise.

It is helpful to have Appendix 7.1 to hand while undertaking the activities in this chapter.

Identifying potential big ideas

National curriculum documents provide a great starting point for identifying your big ideas. For example, in the English national curriculum,

DOI: 10.4324/9781003486589-16

the concept of processes is explicitly found in the programme of study for science and art and design. However, it is easy to see how this concept could also apply to subjects such as design and technology (the process of making) and geography (the processes of changing landscapes). Therefore, the concept of processes is likely a good choice for a big idea.

If you are not required to follow a national curriculum, then subject-association websites or subject-specific textbooks are great places to seek inspiration. In either, case, the following task is a great starting point to elicit people's thoughts and ideas. It is an idea for a staff meeting or a professional development day.

    Task

Organise staff into small working groups and provide them with highlighter pens and copies of national curriculum documentation or other academic texts. Ask each group to highlight concepts they feel fit the characteristics of big ideas (refer to Appendix 7.1 for these).

Ask staff to work through the documentation, writing their suggestions for big ideas on large sheets of paper before sharing them with the other groups. This will build a picture of potential big ideas for your curriculum. Overall, it would help if you aimed to agree on five to ten big ideas.

Figure 10.1 shows a selection of big ideas you can refer to when developing your own, but remember, yours should help you deliver the aims of your curriculum vision.

Defining your big ideas

Once you have identified your potential big ideas, discussing what they mean for your curriculum is vital. As you do this, you should create working definitions for each big idea. Your definitions can be short or extended as shown in Figures 10.2 and 10.3. As you write your descriptions, you may

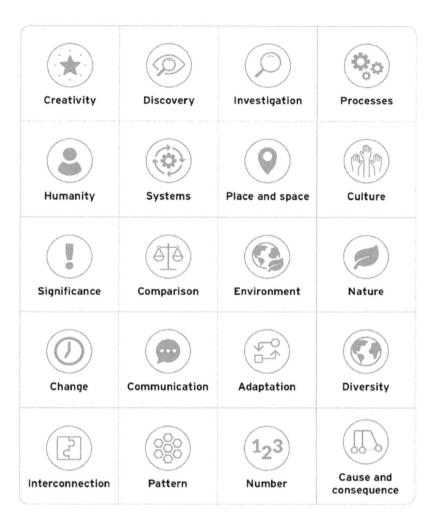

Creativity	Discovery	Investigation	Processes
Humanity	Systems	Place and space	Culture
Significance	Comparison	Environment	Nature
Change	Communication	Adaptation	Diversity
Interconnection	Pattern	Number	Cause and consequence

Figure 10.1 Example big ideas.

find that some potential big ideas are so similar that you want to combine them to make one broader concept. For example, the concepts of investigation and exploration could be combined to form the larger concept of discovery.

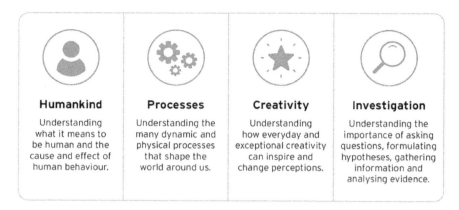

Humankind	**Processes**	**Creativity**	**Investigation**
Understanding what it means to be human and the cause and effect of human behaviour.	Understanding the many dynamic and physical processes that shape the world around us.	Understanding how everyday and exceptional creativity can inspire and change perceptions.	Understanding the importance of asking questions, formulating hypotheses, gathering information and analysing evidence.

Figure 10.2 Examples of short definitions of big ideas.

   Task

Ask staff to work in groups to write short definitions for your big ideas. If, during the process, you find that some big ideas need adapting, discarding or adding in, don't worry; this is a normal part of the process and should be welcomed. Remember you are aiming for five to ten big ideas, so keep this in mind as you refine your definitions.

Editing and checking

You will need to ensure that the definitions of your big ideas are consistent in style and length and read as though they belong to the same curriculum. You should also ensure that the technical vocabulary included in your definitions reinforces the subjects and concepts within each big idea. Table 10.1 provides an example of the use of language in the big ideas of creativity and processes.

Finally, ensure that the big ideas align with your vision for your curriculum. For example, if one of the principles of your curriculum is to have an enquiry-led curriculum, then you would look to include the big ideas of investigation, enquiry and creativity. You may not always be able to make explicit links between the two, but your big ideas should at least be in the spirit of your curriculum vision.

Humankind

Understanding what it means to be human and the cause and effect of human behaviour.

This big idea invites children to find out what it means to be human, including the workings of human anatomy and how to keep safe. They examine ways that the human race is interconnected and explore the human experience and identities through a range of subject lenses. They discover the cause and effect of human behaviour and develop an understanding of the relationships between individuals, societies, faiths and communities. Through this big idea, children discover the ancient secrets of past civilisations and see the multitude of ways in which they influence modern-day life.

Processes

Understanding the many dynamic and physical processes that shape the world around us.

This big idea invites children to find out about the diverse and dynamic physical processes that are present in, and have a significant impact on, places, the environment and the world around them. They explore the physics of force and movement and investigate the phenomena of electricity, light and sound. Through this big idea, children discover how physical processes, such as weather and erosion, can transform a place or landscape.

Creativity

Understanding how everyday and exceptional creativity can inspire and change perceptions.

This big idea invites children to discover the place of everyday and exceptional creativity, including the qualities of persistence, determination, originality and resilience that form the basis of the creative process. They explore ways in which their ideas and imaginings can be realised and communicated and pursue enquiry by asking questions and finding connections between seemingly separate ideas. Through this big idea, children develop an appreciation of the importance of experimentation, trial and error, original thought and self-expression.

Investigation

Understanding the importance of asking questions, formulating hypotheses, gathering information and analysing evidence.

This big idea invites children to be curious and search for answers in response to original, familiar and more complex questions. They explore ways to create hypotheses, gather evidence and begin to evaluate data. They experiment with different ways to present information and ideas and make informed choices to solve problems. Through this big idea, children start to think critically, make meaningful connections and reflect thoughtfully on evidence and ideas.

Figure 10.3 Examples of extended definitions of big ideas.

Table 10.1 Vocabulary for the big ideas of creativity and processes

Big idea: creativity	Big idea: processes
Persistence	Dynamic
Determination	Physical
Originality	Explore
Resilience	Transform
Explore	Force
Ideas	Movement
Imagination	Investigate
Original thought	Phenomena
Self-expression	Discover
Artistic	Geographical
Design	Scientific

Summary

After working through this chapter, you will have chosen the big ideas for your curriculum and discussed and defined them with your colleagues so everyone understands their purpose and meaning. You will have ensured that there are obvious links between your big ideas and your curriculum vision.

You will have checked for consistency in language and writing style and ensured that the big ideas and their definitions provide an academic aspiration for your curriculum.

Well done – this is excellent work! You may revisit your big ideas as you further develop, or continue to improve your curriculum. For now, your big ideas will provide a good starting point for identifying or clarifying your curriculum's subject concepts.

11

IDENTIFYING YOUR SUBJECT CONCEPTS

With your big ideas in place, you can now begin to identify the subject concepts of your curriculum. The subject concepts you choose will connect to your big ideas and help you determine the core knowledge of your curriculum. This chapter suggests practical ways to generate your subject concepts and shows you how to present this information in a series of subject maps.

The work in this chapter is best done in collaboration with subject leaders so there is an ongoing dialogue, a sharing of expertise, cross-referencing between subjects and opportunities for professional debate. The examples in this chapter focus on geography; however, the same process applies to any subject.

It is helpful to have Appendix 7.2 to hand while undertaking the activities in this chapter.

Identifying and refining your subject concepts

Before you begin to identify the subject concepts of your curriculum, you will need to, along with your subject leaders, recap the big ideas of your

DOI: 10.4324/9781003486589-17

curriculum and their definitions. Once you have done this, by either doing one subject at a time or taking multiple subjects, you can start thinking about how each big idea will link to the subject concepts of each curriculum subject. The following task provides a simple method for doing this and is another excellent activity to do during a staff meeting or professional development day.

 Task

Write each big idea on A3 paper and lay them out in an accessible space. Provide each subject leader with sticky notes (it helps if each subject has a different colour) and a marker pen. Ask subject leaders to visit each big idea and consider which concepts of their subject might link.

For example, if your geography subject leader visits the big idea of investigation, they might want to link to it, the geographical concept of fieldwork. Whereas if the science subject leader visits that big idea they may link it to scientific investigation.

Keep this activity going until all subject leaders have visited each big idea. An example of this activity is shown in Figure 11.1.

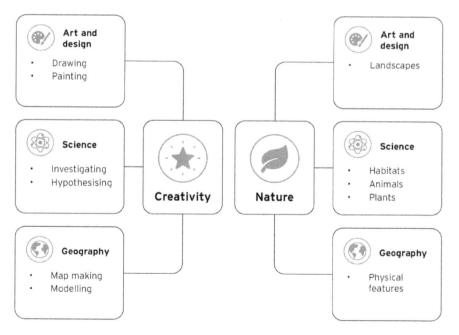

Figure 11.1 Matching subject concepts to big ideas.

Throughout the process, subject leaders should refer to relevant documentation to ensure they have covered everything required. For example, if you follow a national curriculum, subject leaders should reference their subject's programmes of study to ensure that the subject concepts they choose will provide coverage of any statutory requirements.

If there are any anomalous subject concepts that leaders feel are important but don't link to a big idea, ask them to put them to one side to revisit later. Alternatively, if there is a big idea with no subject concepts applied, consider excluding or combining that big idea with another to form a larger and broader big idea.

It is usual for this process to take some time as you try out different combinations and refine your thinking. For many, this task is about generating initial ideas and returning to them later to consolidate, even revisiting them several times. Leave your workings for a few days before returning with fresh eyes to review and refine.

When you return to your initial ideas, you should allow time to discuss the outcomes with subject leaders and listen to those who want to make changes or have ideas for improvement. This will also enable the group to see whether all subjects have balance and equity. For example, ensuring that there are not too many concepts in one subject and too few in another is essential.

However, if you use national curriculum documentation, some subjects will naturally have more programmes of study to cover than others. For example, science will inevitably have more programmes of study to cover than art and design. When there are more programmes of study to cover, the number of concepts the subject leader chooses is likely to reflect this. How many concepts you want across the board and for each subject is up to you, and again, this might be a matter of discussion and debate among colleagues.

If you have put some concepts aside to come back to, you should now decide what you want to do with them. That is, do you want to include or discard them?

Creating subject maps

When subject leaders have identified and linked the concepts of their subject to the big ideas, they can begin to build their subject maps. Eventually, these will combine to form your curriculum progression framework.

	A	B	C	D	E	F	G	H	I
1	Big idea	Subject concept	Aspect	Y1	Y2	Y3	Y4	Y5	Y6
2									
3									
4									
5									
6									
7									
8									
9									
10									
11									
12									
13									
14									

| ◄ ► | Geography | Art and design | Design and technology | Computing | History |

Figure 11.2 Subject map template.

To format subject maps, it is best to use collaborative spreadsheet software. I recommend a template similar to the one shown in Figure 11.2, as this allows subject leaders to show how their concepts link to the big ideas of your curriculum. You will need to duplicate the spreadsheet template in multiple tabs, one for each subject. Add your big ideas to each subject tab and in the same order it will look consistent and save subject leaders' time.

    Task

Ask each subject leader to populate the template with their subject's concepts. These should reflect the previous task and link each concept to a big idea. After a first attempt, allow them to share and compare their work. Encourage the subject leaders to consider if there is a balance across all subjects and if the concepts chosen are a suitable means of delivering the big ideas of your curriculum. It is not essential for every subject to link to every big idea. Try to avoid making tenuous or arbitrary links.

Identify where there might be good opportunities for links across multiple subjects. For example, rocks and soils might be part of the geography

	A	B	C	D	E	F	G	H	I
1	**Big idea**	**Subject concept**	**Aspect**	**Y1**	**Y2**	**Y3**	**Y4**	**Y5**	**Y6**
2	Nature	Physical features							
3	Place and space	The world							
4		Mapping							
5		Location							
6		Direction							
7	Significance	Significant places							
8	Change	Geographical phenomena							
9	Humankind	Human geography							
10	Processes	Physical processes							
11	Creativity	Geographical communication							
12	Investigation	Fieldwork							
13	Materials	Rocks and soils							
14	Comparison	Geographical comparison							
	◄ ►	**Geography**	Art and design		Design and technology		Computing		History

Figure 11.3 Subject map plus geography concepts.

and science subject maps. Subject leaders should collaborate in such cases to decide how this might work – for example, determining how the concept is distinct in each subject and what that means for the next steps of their curriculum planning.

After completing this task, the subject map for geography, for example, might look like Figure 11.3. Remember, this is only an example and may not reflect your choice of big ideas or subject concepts. The concepts you choose should reflect your big ideas and what you feel is most important for each subject.

Once each subject leader has added their subject's concepts to their map, you may want to refine these further into aspects, sometimes called second-order concepts. Aspects help to break down concepts into smaller, more granular parts. An example of this is the concept of physical features in geography, which can break down into aspects of climate zones, biomes and vegetation belts; rivers, mountains, volcanoes and earthquakes; and oceans and seas, as seen in Figure 11.4. Some concepts may not need breaking down into aspects.

	A	B	C	D	E	F	G
1	**Big idea**	**Subject concept**	**Aspect**	**Y1**	**Y2**	**Y3**	**Y4**
2	Nature	Physical features	Climate zones, biomes and vegetation belts				
3			Rivers, mountains, volcanoes and earthquakes				
4			Oceans and seas				
5	Place and space	The world	Countries and continents				
6		Mapping	Map reading				
7			Grid references and coordinates				
8			Aerial photographs and digital mapping				
9		Location					
10		Direction					
11	Significance	Significant places	Terrestrial and marine				
12			Hot and cold				
13	Change	Geographical phenomena	Spatial variation				
14			Change over time				
15	Humankind	Human geography	People and diversity				
16			Settlements and land use				
17	Processes	Physical processes	Weather and the seasons				
18	Creativity	Geographical communication	Writing at length				
19			Geographical vocabulary				
20	Investigation	Fieldwork	Data				
21			Maps				
22	Materials	Rocks and soils					
23	Comparison	Geographical comparison					
	◀ ▶ **Geography**	Art and design	Design and technology	Computing		History	

Figure 11.4 Subject map plus geography aspects.

Task

If you want to break your subject concepts into aspects, ask your leaders to record them, as shown in Figure 11.3. Ensure subject leaders can access the internet, textbooks and national curriculum documentation to help them with this task, especially if they are not specialists. It is important to remember that the more aspects you have, the more detailed your curriculum progression framework will be.

If you decide not to break your subject concepts into aspects, then it can be helpful to elaborate on each concept with an explanation. This will help subject leaders and teachers select the appropriate knowledge and skills for each concept as you develop your curriculum progression framework. Figure 11.5 provides an example of how this might look.

	A	B	C
1	**Big idea**	**Subject concept**	**Explanation**
2	Nature	Physical features	This concept includes climate zones, biomes, vegetation belts and other physical features, including mountains, volcanoes and earthquakes. Oceans, seas, rivers and other water features are also covered by this concept.
3	Place and space	The world	This concept includes study of the world's continents and countries.
4		Mapping	This concept includes study of aerial photographs and plan perspectives to recognise landmarks and basic human and physical features. Learning how to devise and use a simple map; and use and construct basic symbols in a key. Also includes using the eight points of a compass, and four- and six-figure grid references, including on Ordnance Survey maps.
5		Location	The study of the location and characteristics of countries and capital cities. Includes reading maps to locate the world's countries and their environmental regions, key physical and human features and land-use patterns.
6		Direction	The study of simple compass directions (north, south, east and west) and locational and directional language, for example, near and far, left and right, to describe the location of features and routes on a map.
7	Significance	Significant places	The study of significant places both terrestrial and marine. It includes identifying the position and significance of hot and cold places, the equator, the North and South Poles, latitude, longitude, the Northern and Southern Hemispheres, the Tropics of Cancer and Capricorn, the Arctic and Antarctic Circle, the Prime/Greenwich Meridian and time zones (including day and night).
8	Change	Geographical phenomena	The study of geographical phenomena, such as precipitation, temperature, extreme weather, drought, population, deforestation and urbanisation. It explores how environments change over time due to these phenomena.
9	Humankind	Human geography	The study of people, population and diversity, including types of settlement and land use; economic activity, including trade links; and the distribution of natural resources, including energy, food, minerals and water.
10	Processes	Physical processes	The study of weather, the seasons and seasonal and daily weather patterns.
11	Creativity	Geographical communication	The study of geographical information in reports and case studies includes problem solving and reasoning.
12	Investigation	Fieldwork	The study of observing human and physical features in the local area. Includes using methods, such as sketch maps, plans, graphs and digital technologies.
13	Materials	Rocks and soils	The study of the rocks and soils found in different climate zones, biomes and vegetation belts and how this impacts on land use.
14	Comparison	Geographical comparison	The study of the similarities and differences in human and physical geography including local, regional and global locations.

| ◄ ► | **Geography** | Art and design | Design and technology | Computing | History |

Figure 11.5 Subject map with geography explanations.

Checking coverage

Once subject leaders have created their individual subject maps it is important, if you are required to cover a national curriculum, to check you have covered all the necessary or statutory programmes of study.

In some cases, and I would recommend it, subject leaders should add these to their subject maps. An easy way to do this is to create a code for each programme of study and add this into the subject map.

Summary

Together, you will have discussed how well the chosen subject concepts will help you deliver your curriculum's big ideas and will have checked for balance across all subjects. Where you think it is appropriate, you'll have broken subject concepts into smaller aspects or explanations, which will help subject leaders select the right knowledge and skills for your progression framework and help teachers understand each concept's distinct nature.

Great work! In the next chapter, you can use these individual subject maps to help create your curriculum progression framework.

12

BUILDING YOUR CURRICULUM PROGRESSION FRAMEWORK

Having already created your subject maps, subject leaders can now begin adding the appropriate core knowledge for each subject's concepts and aspects. These subject maps will combine to form your curriculum progression framework when complete. As with the previous chapter, examples and appendices are geography-focused, although all tasks and guidance can apply to any subject.

It is helpful to have Appendix 7.3 to hand while undertaking the activities in this chapter.

Types of knowledge

As explained in Chapter 2, there are different types of knowledge. These include substantive, procedural, disciplinary, core and hinterland. In most cases, hinterland knowledge is integrated into teaching resources where additional context is given to engage children and broaden their knowledge base. Adding hinterland knowledge to your framework would be far too

DOI: 10.4324/9781003486589-18

unwieldy and unnecessary. The knowledge you choose for your framework becomes the core knowledge of your curriculum, whether substantive or procedural. Disciplinary knowledge is more likely to be integrated into your procedural knowledge statements and be developed across your curriculum subjects rather than written as specific statements.

Vocabulary

As subject leaders build their subject maps, they must use the correct subject-specific vocabulary. This ensures that teachers and children use the right subject-specific vocabulary in their teaching and learning. Appendix 12.1 provides an example of subject-specific terms for geography.

Selecting and sequencing core knowledge

Subject leaders must make crucial decisions about what knowledge to include and leave out of their subject maps. This requires careful consideration and reflective thinking based on your curriculum's overarching aims, big ideas and subject concepts. Encouraging subject leaders to use subject-specific textbooks, specialist subject sites, and national curriculum documents can help them identify the knowledge needed in the framework.

As subject leaders select core knowledge, they will need to think about how it is sequenced. Remember, A needs to come before B to understand C. As subject leaders carry out this work, they should be mindful of the sequence in which knowledge is placed in the framework. They will also need to consider whether any knowledge needs to be revisited and at what point this should happen within the framework.

  Task

Provide your subject leaders with these questions. Ask them to choose one concept or aspect and map out the core knowledge children need to understand it, and record it on their subject map. If you use a national curriculum, subject leaders should refer to it, as they build their knowledge statements.

1. What core knowledge do children need to understand this concept or aspect?
2. What knowledge comes first?

3. What knowledge comes next?
4. Should this knowledge be revisited? Where?
5. Does the knowledge selected cover the statutory requirements of the national curriculum?
6. Is there a clear progression of knowledge in this concept or aspect from Year 1 to Year 6?
7. Does the chosen core knowledge help children reach our curriculum's end points or big ideas?

Once subject leaders have done this for one concept or aspect, share and compare their outcomes and discuss any issues arising. Once you have ironed out any problems, subject leaders can repeat the exercise for other concepts and aspects.

Writing style

Make sure you agree on the best writing style for your knowledge statements, too. A typical approach is to use active verbs for procedural knowledge. For example, words such as identify, locate, map and analyse are commonly used in geography and also describe some of the disciplinary attributes of geography. Substantive knowledge statements, on the other hand, are often written simply as a fact. For example – a map is a picture or drawing of an area of land or sea.

It is also essential to ensure that knowledge statements are specific enough to be meaningful yet not so detailed that they make teaching, learning or assessing them impossible. Figure 12.1 offers an example of these principles applied to map reading in geography.

 Task

As subject leaders work on their plans, encourage them to discuss, compare and collaborate on the use of language and style. Take time to make improvements and changes to achieve coherence and consistency across all subjects.

Evaluating your curriculum progression framework

As each subject map is completed, your curriculum progression framework will begin to come together as one cohesive document. This is an excellent

	A	B	C	D	E	F	G	H	I
1	Big idea	Subject concept	Aspect	Y1	Y2	Y3	Y4	Y5	Y6
2	Place and space	Mapping	Map reading	A map is a picture or drawing of an area of land or sea.	Physical and human features are represented using symbols on a map. Symbols are organised in a key.	The four cardinal points on a compass are north, south, east and west. These points help us to know the direction we are travelling. A route is a set of directions that can be used to get from one place to another.	Grid lines are used on a map to help locate a place or feature on a map. The vertical lines are called eastings. The horizontal lines are called northings	A 'relief' map describes the difference between the highest and lowest elevations of an area above sea level. Contour lines that are close together represent ground that is steep. Contour lines that are far apart show ground that is gently sloping or flat.	Latitudes are horizontal lines that measure distance north or south of the equator. Longitudes are vertical lines that measure east or west of the meridian in Greenwich, England. Together, latitude and longitude enable cartographers, geographers and others to locate points or places on a map or globe.
				Make and use simple maps Represent places and journeys, real and imagined.	Draw or read a simple picture map using symbols and a key.	Use simple compass directions to describe or follow a route between two locations on a map.	Find a feature or location on a map using grid references.	Identify elevated areas, depressions and river basins on a relief map.	Use lines of latitude and longitude on maps and globes to understand and record the geography of an area.
	Geography	Art and design	Design and technology	Computing	History	Music	Science	Physical education	English

Figure 12.1 Example knowledge statements.

point to share your framework with other stakeholders, such as teachers, asking them to consider its sequencing, progression, use of language, and overall effectiveness. Staff should also reflect upon the body of knowledge specific to their year group to see if it is cohesive, age-appropriate and connects meaningfully with other subjects. You will also need to reflect on how well the concepts, aspects and core knowledge you have included in your framework will help children understand the big ideas of your curriculum.

The effectiveness of your curriculum progression framework will become evident in the longer term as it is taught and assessed. However, there are some things you can do in the shorter term to gauge its effectiveness. Appendix 12.2 provides a range of questions to use when reviewing your framework's progression, sequencing and content.

Summary

This chapter has guided you to create a comprehensive progression framework to underpin your curriculum. Your framework will support teachers to know what core knowledge to teach and help your children understand the concepts and aspects of your curriculum. It should also ensure that your curriculum allows children to progress in their learning over time towards the goals or end points of your curriculum.

This work may have taken some time, but it is crucial to your curriculum's overall effectiveness. Now this is done, you can move on to the next, more imaginative phase of your work, creating your subject narratives.

13

CREATING YOUR CURRICULUM NARRATIVE

After lots of structural and analytical work, this chapter requires you and your teachers to use your imagination to create the narrative of your curriculum. It is best to begin by developing the narrative of one subject before repeating the process for other subjects. Eventually, subject narratives will come together to form the overarching story of your entire curriculum. As history already has an inherent chronology, it is an excellent subject to illustrate the process and exemplify various teaching points.

Choosing topics

Once you decide which subject to do first, teachers can begin to identify topics they need or want to cover in each year group. This task is easier if you follow a national curriculum, as it will already set out any statutory content you need to cover. If you do not follow a national curriculum, you will have greater freedom to choose the topics you want to teach. Encourage staff to refrain from simply choosing topics they are familiar

DOI: 10.4324/9781003486589-19

Table 13.1 Ideas for historical topics

5–7 years	7–11 years
Homes of the past	Greeks
Childhood – then and now	Tudors
Changes in our local community	Victorians
Significant people	Romans
Stone Age to Iron Age	Ancient dynasties
Time and chronology	Invasion and settlement
Toys through time	Democracy and power
Kings and queens	Ancient civilisations
Significant events (of the last 100 years)	Crime and punishment
Travel and leisure – then and now	Medicine through the ages
Samuel Pepys and the Great Fire of London	War and conflict
Local history topics (castles, settlements, significant buildings, etc.)	Local history topics (castles, settlements, significant buildings, etc.)

with and take the opportunity to make some inspiring changes. Looking at each subject map will also help teachers consider what topic or themes will best help deliver the concepts and knowledge of your curriculum. Table 13.1 provides examples of typical historical topics for inspiration.

   Task

Choose your focus subject. Ask each year group to think about the topics they need or want to cover, either as a national curriculum requirement or otherwise. Make sure teachers have access to the chosen subject's map so they can see how topics can be the vehicle to teach the relevant concepts and knowledge.

Ask each year group to write each topic (and a brief description of what it might include) on a separate sheet of paper. When complete, ask staff to lay their topics in sequence from Year 1 to Year 6 so you can see how your narrative will progress over time. Work collaboratively to review each year group's choices and discuss where they could make meaningful connections and flashbacks.

Sequencing your narrative

Once staff have sequenced their topics across the year groups and considered each topic's viability, they will need to consider the sequence they will teach them within each year group.

As they do this, they can begin to plot each project on a medium-term plan. They will need to consider how many weeks each topic might last, for example, over a 6-week or 12-week period. Of course, this depends on the concepts and content covered in each project; as some may need to be taught in more depth (and require more time), while some might be taught more succinctly in less time. At this stage, it is more about sequencing the narrative rather than the details.

Table 13.2 shows a typical medium-term plan for the subject of history. You can see that each year group has made decisions about where and when to teach each topic and how long it will take. It is also evident in this plan that the school has made a series of important decisions. For example, you can see that in Years 1, 2 and 3, the history topics are taught over approximately six weeks and are planned in alternate half terms. By spacing their history topics like this, teachers can better manage the distribution of historical resources and allow for periods of retrieval when they are not introducing new content.

In Years 4, 5 and 6, the school has chosen to teach three longer history topics each lasting a full term. This is likely because of the amount of historical content teachers need to teach and to allow older children time to study their topics more deeply.

This clearly shows the school's history narrative over the course of their entire curriculum. If asked to explain their narrative, a Y1 teacher might say:

> In Y1 children begin their history narrative by studying their family history. It includes an introduction to timelines, chronology and historical terms such as past and present, long ago, before and after, then and now. In the spring term children expand their historical thinking to

Table 13.2 A typical medium-term plan for the subject of history

Year group	Half term 1	Half term 2	Half term 3	Half term 4	Half term 5	Half term 6
Year 1	My family, my history		Toys through time		The Great Fire of London	
Year 2		Childhood then and now		Kings and Queens		Life in a castle
Year 3	Stone Age to Iron Age		Romans		Saxons and Vikings	
Year 4	Ancient Egypt		Local history study		The Victorians	
Year 5	Local history study		Shang Dynasty		Ancient Greece	
Year 6	Benin		Second World War		Local history study	

find out how toys have changed beyond living memory, including how materials, technology and family life has influenced how and what children play with. This project includes a visit to the local museum to see examples of toys from the Victorian era. In the summer term children learn about the fire of London, understanding how significant events can impact people's lives and places. It requires the children to delve more deeply into history from long ago (1666).

Asking each year group to draft a narrative statement is a nice way of getting them to think about what they are teaching and in what order. It is also a good thing to have in place for inspection.

Appendix 13.1 provides example templates for your medium-term plan.

Turning topics into projects

A project provides a structure for a topic and includes the lessons and learning activities that help teachers teach the content, concepts, knowledge and skills of your curriculum. Some schools require teachers to create brief project overviews, such as shown in Figure 13.1 while others require their teachers to create more detailed lesson plans.

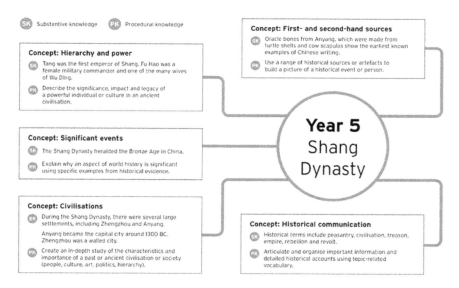

Figure 13.1 Year 5 Shang Dynasty project outline example.

For more detailed planning, teachers should think of each project as having a start point, a deep and rich middle, and a strong ending. This will help them to consider the sequence of their lessons so that new knowledge and skills build on prior learning. They will also need to think about your school's chosen pedagogy in their lesson plans. You might ask them, for example, 'How will your lessons be planned according to our chosen pedagogy?' and 'What strategies and teaching methodologies will you use to teach the planned activities?'

To ensure maximum connectivity and robustness, it is helpful for teachers to identify the big idea, concept, aspect, knowledge or skill for each lesson. This information can be easily taken from your curriculum progression framework.

Appendix 13.2 provides a blank template for more detailed planning and Appendix 13.3 provides a completed project plan for a Y2 history project.

Ultimately, the level of detail you want for your project planning is down to your school preference and the experience and confidence of the teachers but when introducing a new curriculum, it is worth asking teachers to do some form of lesson planning, however brief, until things become a little better embedded.

   Task

Ask teachers to work in their year group teams and choose one topic to begin drafting as a more structured project. You can share Appendix 13.3 as a worked example for reference.

Naming projects

When the content and focus of a project are explicit you can name it. There are different ways to name your projects, from the straightforward approach, for example, 'The Romans', to a more thought-provoking approach, for example, 'What did the Romans do for us?'. While a straightforward approach is a more traditional approach to naming curriculum projects, using a question can help promote children's sense of curiosity about what the project entails. Table 13.3 provides examples of project names.

Table 13.3 Examples of project names

Straight forward	Enquiry
The Romans in Britain	What did the Romans do for Britain?
The Victorians	How did the Industrial Revolution change the world?
Stone Age to Iron Age	How did Britain change from the Stone Age to the Iron Age?
Second World War	How did the Second World War change Britain?
Kings and Queens of Britain	Who was the greatest monarch in British history?

    Task

Ask staff to explore different options for naming their curriculum projects. Encourage them to share their ideas and be consistent in their approach, thinking how well the titles of their projects reflect the narrative. Each year group can add their project names to the medium-term plan.

Evaluating your narrative

Once you are happy that you have a consistent approach to developing your projects – you can continue to develop one subject entirely. It is important to see how projects scan across each year group and the whole school. Ask yourself: What story does this [subject] tell throughout our curriculum? Does it help our children understand the important aspects of [subject]? Appendix 13.4 will help guide you through this process. Address any gaps, duplication, progression or sequencing issues with teachers, with the support of each subject leader. It is also important at this point to see if there are any opportunities for links to be made between subject narratives.

Summary

By the end of this chapter, you may have one or more subject narratives drafted. This should include curriculum projects with a series of sequenced lesson plans that link your big ideas, concepts, knowledge and skills of your curriculum. If you are happy with the standards of projects across school and the narrative of your first subject is effective and well-sequenced, you can decide whether to move on to the next chapter and create resources for your planned projects or repeat this process for other subjects.

This is a significant undertaking, and reaching this point in your curriculum development work is a real achievement. Well done!

14

CURATING YOUR CURRICULUM RESOURCES

By now, you will have begun to build the subject narratives of your curriculum. As your narratives develop, so will your projects and teachers need to consider what resources they will need to teach them.

We have already discussed the importance and different types of resources you will need to teach your curriculum in Appendix 7.5. This chapter focuses on developing bespoke knowledge organisers for your curriculum projects.

Getting started

It is useful for each project to have a knowledge organiser. This will add some consistency to the resourcing of your curriculum and provide a valuable point of information for teachers, children, parents and carers. If you are planning your subject narratives one at a time, creating knowledge organisers for that narrative is advisable before moving on to the next. This will help teachers be in the flow of that subject and see how knowledge organisers progress throughout the school.

DOI: 10.4324/9781003486589-20

In this chapter, examples come from the subjects of art and design and design and technology; however, the same process applies to all subjects of your curriculum.

Familiarisation

Before starting to make your knowledge organisers, it is vital for all staff to know:

- what they are
- how they are used
- their typical features
- why quality matters
- the misconceptions and pitfalls of poor use

 Task

Ask all teachers to read Appendix 14.1, which provides a comprehensive overview of the bulleted points.

Planning your knowledge organisers

If staff have not created knowledge organisers before, it is worth asking them to work in their year group teams to plan one collaboratively. This will help resolve any issues and allow you to iron out any problems. Appendix 14.2 provides a blank template for creating knowledge organisers. The following task provides guidance for using the template.

 Task

1. Choose a topic or project. Write its name in the title box.
2. Add the core knowledge into the core knowledge box. If you have a lot of core knowledge, you should streamline it a little to not overwhelm the reader.
3. Add any subject-specialist vocabulary to the vocabulary box. This can eventually be expanded into a glossary if required.
4. List any images, tables, diagrams and illustrations you want to include on your knowledge organiser. Remember to check copyright laws, as using prohibited images may cause problems later.

5. Add any other contextual knowledge in the hinterland knowledge box. Think about what is appropriate to broaden children's understanding and add interest. Getting the balance right here is vital to prevent overwhelming the reader.
6. Timelines are brilliant for adding detail to knowledge organisers, as are charts, tables and the like, for showing data. Using quotes is also a nice touch; many are freely available online. Use the final two boxes to make a note of any of these features.

Once staff's plans are complete, it is important to fact-check everything, even if it is copied from your progression framework. Sloppy copy-and-paste accidents can ruin an otherwise accurate document. When you are happy that the knowledge organisers are developing correctly, you can move on to their design.

Designing your knowledge organisers

When teachers are clear on the information they want to include in their knowledge organisers, you must consider how you want to design them. For example, you may decide to use an agreed format or you may prefer to allow year groups to make their own choices about how the knowledge organisers are designed. A consistent approach is much better for children, as they are familiar with the format and how to use them. However, as children age, the knowledge organisers will likely be more complex due to the amount of knowledge, images and graphics needed to present the information. Appendix 14.3 provides an example of art and design knowledge organiser for a drawing and design project 'Ammonite' and a design and technology knowledge organisers for a food project 'Food for Life'.

Making your knowledge organisers

Making your knowledge organisers can be a huge administrative undertaking. It can be worth allocating non-contact time for senior leaders to do this based on teacher's plans. It is possible to purchase knowledge organisers, but they won't necessarily reflect the core knowledge of your curriculum.

Learning with knowledge organisers

Knowledge organisers are a crucial part of helping children know and remember more, and they form an integral part of any well-sequenced curriculum. The success of your knowledge organisers can be judged by how well they help children to know and remember more; however, you will have to monitor this over time, and you should plan to carry out activities to observe children using them in their day-to-day learning. You might also want to get parents' feedback on how useful they are in supporting children's home learning.

Summary

By the end of this chapter, all stakeholders should be familiar with the benefits and features of a good knowledge organiser and will have begun to plan and make some examples (one subject at a time is best).

Developing a full suite of knowledge organisers will take time. Once your approach and design are decided, teachers will become more confident and competent in making them and children in using them.

Make sure to collect examples from different year groups to ensure consistent quality, and consider how you will monitor their use and impact over time.

Great work. Now, you can move on to the final chapter of this phase of your curriculum development work – creating low-stake quizzes to support the assessment of your curriculum.

15

ASSESSMENT

By now, you will have developed or improved most of your curriculum. This chapter provides guidance on developing low-stakes quizzes, which can form a valuable part of your integral assessment practice.

You should enable teachers to lead on this, with support from your assessment and subject leaders. However, as with all your other curriculum development work, it is crucial to take an overview to ensure quality and consistency across the school.

This chapter focuses on developing low-stakes quizzes for science but you can apply the same process to the making of quizzes for other subjects.

Tests or quizzes

The terms test and quiz are often used interchangeably, but they are distinct. Tests are typically seen as a more formal way of assessing children's learning, often used at the end of a project and cover more content. Quizzes are shorter and less formal and focus on the content or skills taught

DOI: 10.4324/9781003486589-21

in a lesson or lessons. Used frequently, a quiz can help teachers to quickly identify gaps or misconceptions in children's learning.

Quizzes tend to assess knowledge predominantly, as they are often used to quickly check facts and information learned in a lesson. In a test, children can be expected to be assessed on their recall of substantive and procedural knowledge.

Deciding what to assess

Whether you are creating quizzes, tests or both to assess children's learning of your curriculum, they must reflect the core knowledge and skills of the lessons or projects taught. You will have a good head start on this as you should have already identified the core knowledge for each lesson and project.

Critically, when addressing aspects of procedural knowledge in your tests, children should be allowed to use and apply their skills in familiar and new contexts. For example, if children have learned how to read and interpret climate data in the context of a project about the Arctic, they could be asked to read and compare climate data about the Sahara Desert. In doing this, children are being tested on their ability to read and interpret the data rather than knowledge about the Sahara. However, their knowledge of the Arctic climate will support this, and they should be able to draw inferences about the climate of the Sahara using their understanding of the Arctic.

Types of question

Quizzes

Most quizzes use questions which can be answered quickly and are easy to mark. Examples include multiple choice and true and false questions. These types of questions can feel more fun and less threatening for children; hence, they are much lower stakes than formal tests. Appendix 15.1 provides two examples of low-stakes quizzes for science. Note the different types of easy-response questions in use.

 Task

Ask teachers to choose a lesson and draft 10–20 easy-response questions. Artificial intelligence (AI) software can help teachers as a starting point but should always be used with caution. Share and compare teachers' questions and discuss any thoughts, ideas or issues arising.

Tests

Tests often require more extended questions and answers. Appendix 15.2 provides information and examples of test style questions for science. These types of questions should help teachers to see if children have a depth of knowledge and identify those working at greater depth. Tests are generally harder to create in school due to the amount of time and workload required. Therefore, it is worth looking for commercial options that are aligned to the core knowledge of your curriculum.

Answer sheets

Creating answer sheets will help teachers to quickly mark children's tests or quizzes and ensure there is consistency and standardisation in marking and feedback. Although this work may seem time-consuming, it is well worth doing so that any teacher assessments are accurate and informative. Again, creating these with the help of your subject leaders is important for knowing what answers are acceptable or not.

Task

Ask teachers to devise an answer sheet for the quiz they have created. Discuss how you will score, grade and record them without creating an unnecessary administrative burden. For example, you may decide that quizzes can be self-marked, or peer-marked by the children during the lesson and scores checked and recorded by teaching assistants.

Curriculum impact

The purpose of developing quizzes and tests is to assess how well children understand your curriculum. By collecting data from the tests and quizzes, patterns and trends will emerge over time. For example, you may see consistently low marks across the board on the topic of forces. If so, you can analyse your data to see which aspects of this topic children struggle with most and think about how you might need to address them in your curriculum.

Over time, your quizzes and tests should also tell you which children are working at age-related expectations, and which are falling behind. Such targeted information will help your teachers identify children who need additional support to revisit a piece of knowledge, skill, or concept.

Summary

By the end of this chapter, your teachers will have begun to develop your school's approach to assessing children's understanding of your curriculum. You'll have explored ways of writing questions for quizzes and have several prototypes to try with the children. You will also have discussed tests and how you will mark, record, and analyse any data.

Once you have tried out your quizzes, you may want to continue to develop a full suite to accompany your curriculum projects.

Fantastic! Now, you are ready to move on to the fourth phase of your development work. That is, implementing and evaluating aspects of your new or improved curriculum.

PHASE 3: CHECKLIST

THE DESIGN AND CREATE PHASE

You have reached the end of the third phase. During this phase, you will have begun to design aspects of your new or improved curriculum. As part of the process, you will have enabled teachers and subject leaders to create various structures and content for your curriculum using their expertise, creativity and experience. Use this checklist to help you reflect on your work during this phase.

During this phase, you will have:

✓ Agreed on and defined the big ideas for your curriculum.
✓ Worked with subject leaders to create subject maps.
✓ Combined all subject maps to create your curriculum progression framework.
✓ Created a series of engaging curriculum projects for one or more subjects based on your curriculum progression framework.
✓ Made knowledge organisers for some or all of your projects.
✓ Devised a series of quizzes to help teachers assess children's understanding of your curriculum.

DOI: 10.4324/9781003486589-22

PHASE 4: SYNOPSIS

THE IMPLEMENTATION AND EVALUATION PHASE

In this final phase of the book, you'll begin implementing your curriculum and evaluating its impact, consistency and fidelity. This chapter will support you in actioning your new ideas and guide your monitoring and evaluation.

As with the other phases, there are various tasks for you to carry out, either individually or with colleagues. Each is designed to help you think practically and systematically about implementing change and make sound judgements about how things work.

However, it is important to acknowledge that while your curriculum will have some short-term benefits, the fundamental shift will become more evident in the longer term as children progress through the school. Only then will you see the true impact of your curriculum on their learning as they develop new knowledge and understanding over time.

DOI: 10.4324/9781003486589-23

16

IMPLEMENTATION AND EVALUATION

Curriculum implementation refers to the teaching of your planned curriculum. That is, bringing your curriculum to life, off the paper and into the classroom. This final phase enables you to see the fruits of your labour through various monitoring and evaluation activities. These activities will highlight your new or improved curriculum's strengths and areas needing continued development.

Implementing your new or improved curriculum will involve all stakeholders, including senior leaders, governors, teachers, parents and children. Everyone has a vital role in ensuring your plans are effective and sustainable. Teachers, of course, are the foot soldiers of your curriculum's implementation. They will work at the coalface, teaching and assessing whether children are learning or not learning your curriculum. Subject leaders are also a crucial part of the practical implementation of your curriculum. Their role is to ensure that all staff have the knowledge, plans, resources and know-how to teach all subjects confidently. They will need to support teachers both formally and informally and support you with the monitoring and evaluation of the impact of your curriculum.

DOI: 10.4324/9781003486589-24

In this book, you have been encouraged to timeline your developments so that they are completed and introduced in a manageable way. Your plans will provide you with a clear route for implementation without the fear of overwhelming stakeholders.

Whether you are about to teach an entirely new curriculum or, for example, a new history narrative, there are certain things you can do to ensure things run smoothly for all concerned.

Encourage curriculum fidelity

As teachers implement the curriculum, they must keep the fidelity of what you have planned. This includes your curriculum progression framework, concepts, aspects, knowledge and skills. Keeping true to your intended curriculum should ensure its integrity and that any sequencing you have put in place remains. However, while fidelity to your intended plans is important, it will sometimes be necessary for teachers to use their professional judgement and experience to make thoughtful adaptations for those children who need them. Teachers should record their adaptions so that the information can be shared and reflected upon with subject and senior leaders.

Promote communication and collaboration

As teachers implement your new or improved curriculum, they must continue communicating and collaborating. Sharing ideas, discussing feedback and sharing effective teaching strategies are essential to keep everyone informed and motivated. Significantly, this ongoing collaboration will help you ensure that the implementation of your curriculum is consistent across different classrooms, year groups or phases, which is crucial. Communicating with each other and sharing experiences is also a fantastic way of encouraging mutual support and teacher well-being.

Monitor and evaluate

As new aspects of your curriculum become embedded, teachers, subject leaders, and senior leaders need to monitor and evaluate the effectiveness of any changes you have made. This can include work sampling, lesson observations, walk-throughs, test analysis and other pupil assessments. Once you have this evidence, you must work with the necessary staff to address any issues emerging. Ultimately, this can lead you back to Phase 2, perhaps adapting and updating your curriculum development plan.

Monitoring systems

Having adequate monitoring systems alongside effective teaching strategies and purposeful and meaningful assessment practices will be crucial in helping you judge the effectiveness, consistency and fidelity of new or improved curriculum structure and content.

The following paragraphs are a reminder of some of the different activities you may want to do to monitor the implementation of your curriculum.

Data

Collecting and analysing data from teacher assessments, tests, quizzes, surveys, focus groups, classroom observations and discussions will provide you and senior and subject leaders with valuable insight into the impact of your curriculum.

Conferencing

One-to-one or small group conversations with staff and children are valuable monitoring activities and can help you and subject leaders build on those informal daily interactions. Listening to children's thoughts and views about the curriculum also shows that you value and encourage pupil voice.

Work sampling

Work sampling, or book looks, can provide a valuable means of monitoring what children know and can do and seeing what has been taught. It can be helpful to select books from children of different ability levels, especially to see if higher attainers are being challenged and those less able are being well supported. Always have a clear focus for work sampling to avoid being distracted by other aspects of the children's work. For example, if you are looking at children's use of scientific vocabulary, don't stress about other things, such as handwriting or grammar.

Lesson observations

Lesson observations have a terrible reputation, but they are a valuable means of gathering evidence about the curriculum and sharing good practice. It is, therefore, essential to ensure an agreed protocol for carrying out lesson observations to foster a climate of positivity and support for teachers.

Monitoring protocol

When carrying out lesson observations it is best to have an agreed protocol for doing so across the school. This will help all stakeholders understand the process and see it as a shared endeavour they are part of rather than something done to them.

For example, you can agree that any observations are made against agreed criteria, which focus on the subject rather than the quality of teaching. Or that an observation will only last a maximum of 30 minutes.

It is also crucial that any information you gather is discussed with the class teacher or subject leader. Hence, they can respond or add something you missed during any monitoring activity. The aim is for all stakeholders to see the process as constructive and positive as possible and to get the best picture of what is happening rather than being judgemental.

 Task

Discuss the parameters of lesson observations with senior leaders and other stakeholders, such as governors, to agree on a shared and constructive approach. Appendix 16.1 provides a range of templates you can use or adapt for your own purposes.

Evaluating

Once you have carried out a range of monitoring activities, a picture of the impact of your curriculum will begin to emerge. You should also interrogate any data you have so that you can draw accurate conclusions based on evidence. Looking for patterns and trends will help you identify any misconceptions and gaps in children's or teachers' understanding and the successes of your curriculum, too. By analysing and evaluating the evidence you have collected, you can draw conclusions about the impact and effectiveness of your curriculum developments. The following task will assist you in evaluating any evidence you have and knowing what to do.

 Task

Revisit your curriculum development plan and check the evidence you have against your success criteria. Based on your findings, adjustments may need to be made to the curriculum, but it is essential to realise that some things will take longer than others to embed. You can add any adaptations to your curriculum development plan.

You must also communicate your monitoring and evaluation results to all stakeholders. Half-termly or termly meetings, subject leader reports, newsletters, governor reports or parent newsletters are a good way of keeping everyone informed. Appendix 16.2 provides an example of a subject leader's report for history.

Summary

Knowing the impact of your curriculum is crucial for determining whether it is achieving its intended outcomes and meeting the needs of all your children.

However, monitoring and evaluating your curriculum is part of an ongoing cyclical process as set out initially in the Curriculum Development Wheel. Any evidence you collect will feed back into this ongoing curriculum development process, ensuring that your school continually strives to improve your educational provision for all children.

PHASE 4: CHECKLIST

THE IMPLEMENTATION AND EVALUATION PHASE

You have completed the fourth phase of this book. During this phase, you will have begun to implement your new or improved curriculum and begun to monitor and evaluate its impact. Take time now to reflect on this final phase.

During this phase you will have:

✓ Begun to implement your new or improved curriculum using your school's agreed pedagogy.
✓ Carried out some monitoring and evaluation activities aligned with those you outlined in your curriculum development plan.
✓ Begun to reflect on things that are working well and those that require further improvement.
✓ Monitored the implementation of your curriculum to check its fidelity, that is, whether what teachers are teaching meets the intentions of your planned curriculum.

DOI: 10.4324/9781003486589-23

✓ Identified any gaps or misconceptions in your curriculum.
✓ Begun to draw conclusions about the impact of your curriculum on children's learning.
✓ Identified areas for ongoing development.

17

FINAL WORDS

Dear Reader,

Change takes courage as well as resilience, confidence and strategic planning. Change management also requires interpersonal, communication and organisational skills.

The purpose of this book has been to support you through one of the most significant changes you can ever make in school – developing your curriculum. The intent was to simplify that process as much as possible to make it manageable and give you a logical and practical approach. I hope it has helped you make some substantial changes and improvements, even if there is still more work to do.

When you began your curriculum journey, you probably had some ideas about what you wanted to achieve and how you wanted to achieve it. The critical question is, 'Have you achieved what you wanted?'

I hope the answer is 'Yes! Of course!' but if not, don't worry, remember curriculum development is not a linear process but a cyclical one. Go back to the Curriculum Development Wheel and see which phase you might

DOI: 10.4324/9781003486589-25

need to return to, not to start again but to revisit specific aspects of your curriculum that may require further development.

Enjoy watching your curriculum grow and mature. Relish the opportunities to observe children learning new things and soaking up the activities and experiences you've planned for them. Remember to share your successes with stakeholders in and out of the school. Governors, parents, carers and the wider community should know all about your successes and be part of celebrating your achievements. Shouting about your achievements on your school website, writing to parents to share new developments and showcasing children's work through special assemblies or community events are all excellent ways of sharing the fruits of your labours. Furthermore, don't forget to make children's learning visible through wall displays, local press, your school website, and, where appropriate, social media platforms.

Remember, many of the changes you make will take time to embed and for all stakeholders to get used to. If you've documented your journey as you've worked through this book, look back at where you started, and you'll realise just how much work you've done and how much things have improved.

Don't worry if you encounter bumps in the road ahead. Mistakes and challenges are all a normal part of school life and the curriculum development process. While I thank you for your investment in this book and this process, it is essential to acknowledge that even with both our best efforts, real life, with all its unexpected demands, will undoubtedly raise its ugly head to challenge us. School issues such as budget deficits, staff turnover, challenging behaviour and the threat of a pending inspection are all things teachers face daily, as are personal issues such as relationships, work-life balance and well-being.

If you can stay focused on your vision and continue to drive it forward in the face of these challenges, you are a superhero. But remember to give yourself some slack when you need it. Try to feel proud of your work as you reach this final chapter. It is an outstanding achievement.

As I continue to work with primary schools worldwide, I remain struck by the devotion and dedication of primary teachers and leaders who, like you, work hard every day to improve the lives of all children. Even when the challenges are great, primary schools worldwide dedicate themselves to this common cause to provide our children with an excellent standard of education, a right to be heard and a chance of a fulfilling adult life. No one knows better than primary practitioners that if we want to improve the world of tomorrow, then the children of today need our love, attention and the opportunity to study an amazing curriculum.

As I write the final few words of this book, my belief that the curriculum is a powerful tool for positive change is as strong as ever. Continuing to share *Curriculum Simplexity* as a means of achieving this continues to be the focus of my work.

And finally, please do remember to look after yourself and your colleagues. After all, we can only hope to make positive and sustainable changes for others, if we promise to take care of ourselves.

Melanie x

APPENDIX 1.1

THE EARLY YEARS CURRICULUM

The early years are traditionally recognised as the period from birth until children start more formal education. The age at which children begin formal learning varies across different countries and cultures, but typically, the early years range from birth to five. This period of a child's life is arguably the most critical stage of development.

Babies are born ready to learn, and a child's early years are one of rapid growth and development. In fact, by age six, the child's brain has developed to 90% of its adult size.[1] The experiences that children have in their early years lay the foundations for their future.

Curriculum structure in the early years

Unlike the primary curriculum, which is typically planned and taught as specific subjects, an early-year's curriculum generally has broader areas of learning, such as physical development, creative development and communication. While these areas of learning provide a structure for the curriculum, teachers are often able to plan more flexibly to make changes according to children's individual or group needs. If the curriculum allows all children to explore, investigate and begin to understand the world around them, then the structure should not restrict valuable learning experiences as they arise.

Knowledge and skills in the early years curriculum

Any good early years curriculum should help children to develop their understanding of the world and include opportunities for them to develop their skills. The learning experiences teachers offer should enable all children to explore and manipulate materials and sounds, sing songs, paint, draw, construct, communicate, count and create imaginative stories. Such experiences, enable children to establish the building blocks they need for educational achievement and good mental and physical health. It is also important to reflect and respect aspects of the local culture and knowledge, which are deemed important to the local community.

How to build an early years curriculum

Although there is often more flexibility for designing an early years curriculum, it is helpful to follow some simple guidelines and principles. The following paragraphs offer some guidance for developing an early years curriculum.

Have clear curriculum goals

It is vital for anyone tasked with designing an early years curriculum to have a good understanding of child development so they can set appropriate curriculum goals. Such goals should reflect the school's curriculum goals but should be adapted to ensure that they reflect the needs of the school's youngest children. Examples of curriculum goals in relation to the area of learning, Understanding the world, are shown in Table 1.1.

Set out your curriculum's learning steps

Once you have established the goals for your curriculum, you will need to set out the smaller steps children must take to achieve them. These are usually written as smaller incremental statements. Table 1.2 provides an

Table 1.1 Examples of curriculum goals

Areas of learning	Goals
Understanding the world (links to scientific development)	• To understand and describe the yearly changes of the seasons. • To explore the natural world and name and describe familiar plants and animals. • To begin describing observations about forces and natural phenomena, such as magnetism, shadows, reflections and rainbows. • To describe a range of materials and their properties. • To begin to understand and describe scientific processes and changes in state.

Table 1.2 Examples of learning steps

Goal	Birth to 3	3–4 years	4–5 years	5–6 years
To understand and describe the yearly changes of the seasons.	Explore the natural environment and begin to learn vocabulary related to weather and seasonal change.	Notice and talk about how the local environment (including plants, animals and the weather) changes with the seasons.	Name the four seasons (in the United Kingdom) spring, summer, autumn and winter, and begin to describe typical weather associated with each season.	Know that the day length is shorter in the winter and longer in the summer.

example of what this might look like for the curriculum goal, to understand and describe the yearly changes of the seasons.

Consider your pedagogic approach

While having a curriculum plan in place is essential, there is no one right way to teach children in the early years. Each setting is different, and pedagogy is often driven by the needs of the children rather than any top-down or specific approach. However, some early years settings do opt for more specific approaches, such as Reggio Emilia Approach®,[2] Montessori,[3] Froebel,[4] Steiner/Waldorf[5] and Forest school.[6]

In most early years' settings teachers plan themes or projects across the year, to organise the knowledge and skills of the curriculum. Such themes and projects can provide engaging and interesting ways for children to explore popular topics, such as the body, animals, plants, seasons, celebrations, food, traditions and stories.

Plan a wide range of vocabulary

To acquire knowledge, develop creativity and access new learning experiences, children need to learn and understand a wide range of vocabulary. The more vocabulary a child has, the more they can connect with the varied experiences a good curriculum offers. So, it is also crucial for any early years curriculum to offer children multiple and varied opportunities to learn new words, listen to and engage with a wide variety of adults and talk and interact with their peers. In many settings, teachers plan to teach vocabulary that links to particular topics and themes and encourage children to use it in as many different ways as possible. This can include through their play and in enhanced and continuous provision.

Provide a wide range of reading opportunities

Research shows that regularly reading to children is crucial in learning to read. In her book, *Proust and the Squid: The Story and Science of the Reading Brain*,[7] Maryanne Wolf explores how emerging prereaders learn fundamental preliteracy skills when sharing stories with adults. Reading quality stories to children introduces them to a wide range of vocabulary and supports their communication and language skills. The natural conversations that arise when sharing books also develop their understanding and comprehension skills and can foster a love of reading later in life. Therefore, story time must be a priority for all early years' settings. Carefully selected stories can add context to the curriculum and allow children to connect with characters and compare their lives and experiences with others.

Create purposeful environments

Creating a practical, purposeful and playful environment for children to learn in will inevitably support their development across the curriculum. Enhancing the environment with resources that link to a specific theme will allow children to revisit learning independently and build their skills and knowledge. The nurseries and preschools in the Reggio Emilia Approach® view the learning environment as a 'third teacher' alongside parents and classroom teachers.

Knowing your children well and understanding their developmental needs allows you to carefully select appropriate resources that will provide the correct level of challenge. Natural and open-ended resources support and develop children's creativity and imagination. For example, a simple wooden block could be a car, a telephone, an animal or a house!

Cultural considerations

Knowing and understanding children's early experiences and having strong links with their families is essential. The Reggio Emilia Approach® holds parent partnership as crucial to young children's development. The collaboration and interaction between the family, parents and schools are paramount in facilitating the transfer and understanding of each child's experiences and learning needs. This constant dialogue between parents and teachers about the children supports the teachers as they build their curriculum. Providing plenty of opportunities for parents and carers to become part of the children's learning experiences through activities, such as baking, story time, playing games and reading are great ways to develop partnerships with parents and carers.

Communicate with others

To ensure your early years curriculum prepares your children for the next stage of their learning journey, there must be strong communication between early years teachers and primary teachers, especially as children make the transition between Reception and Year one. It is also crucial to ensure that the primary curriculum builds on children's prior learning, and this can only be achieved when there is robust communication about the curriculum between the relevant teachers. Having termly conversations is a commitment but ultimately worth the time if you want to achieve real coherence.

And finally

Building an early years curriculum that nurtures the youngest of children is a crucial part of a school's curriculum development journey. This is so that all children, no matter their starting point, will have an equal opportunity to build the foundations they need to start their learning journey.

In this book, the curriculum development process is both cyclical and ongoing, and this is particularly crucial in the early years. Establishing an annual review of your curriculum will ensure that it takes account of the different starting points for new cohorts of children.

Ultimately, the most important thing to remember is that an excellent early years curriculum has the children's needs, interests and well-being at its heart.

Notes

[1] Tanner, JM. *Foetus Into Man: Physical Growth from Conception to Maturity.* Harvard University Press; 2003.

[2] Reggio Emilia Approach®. Accessed 12 February 2024. https://www.reggiochildren.it/en/reggio-emilia-approach

[3] Association Montessori International. About Montessori. Accessed 12 February 2024. https://montessori-ami.org/about-montessori

[4] Froebel Trust. A Forebelian approach. Accessed 12 February 2024. https://www.froebel.org.uk/uploads/documents/FT-Froebels-principles-and-practice-today.pdf

[5] Steiner/Waldorf. Britannica. History & society. Waldorf school education. Accessed 12 February 2024. https://www.britannica.com/topic/Waldorf-school

[6] Forest School Association. Accessed 12 February 2024. https://forestschoolassociation.org/

[7] Wolf M, Stoodley CJ. *Proust and the Squid: The Story and Science of the Reading Brain.* Icon Books Ltd; 2008.

References

Association Montessori International. About Montessori. Accessed 12 February 2024. https://montessori-ami.org/about-montessori

Forest School Association. Accessed 12 February 2024. https://forestschoolassociation.org/

Froebel Trust. A Forebelian approach. Accessed 12 February 2024. https://www.froebel.org.uk/uploads/documents/FT-Froebels-principles-and-practice-today.pdf

Reggio Emilia Approach®. Accessed 12 February 2024. https://www.reggiochildren.it/en/reggio-emilia-approach

Steiner/Waldorf. Britannica. History & society. Waldorf school education. Accessed 12 February 2024. https://www.britannica.com/topic/Waldorf-school

Tanner JM. *Foetus into Man: Physical Growth from Conception to Maturity*. Harvard University Press; 2003.

Wolf M, Stoodley CJ. *Proust and the Squid: The Story and Science of the Reading Brain*. Icon Books Ltd; 2008.

APPENDIX 3.1

CULTURAL CAPITAL
READING LIST

Understanding Bourdieu (2002) Webb J, Schirato T, Danaher G (SAGE Publications Ltd.)

This book provides a comprehensive and well-thought-out introduction to Bourdieu's work. It is an excellent book for anyone getting to grips with Bourdieu for the first time.

Distinction: a social critique of the judgement of taste (2010) Bourdieu P (Routledge)

In his most famous work, Bourdieu focuses on taste and preference. First published in 1979, this book proposes that our choices are distinctions and are influenced by our social class – choices made in opposition to those made by other classes. Here, Bourdieu argues that those with high social and cultural capital are the arbiters of taste and that our tastes come from our social class.

Pierre Bourdieu: key concepts (2012) Grenfell M (Routledge)

This book highlights Bourdieu's most important concepts in detail. Each chapter focuses on an individual concept and is helpful for anyone wanting foundational knowledge of Bourdieu.

Bourdieu and education (education and social theory) (2020) Reay D (Routledge)

This book is a collection of published papers that put Bourdieu's theories into practice. It includes considerations of educational inequalities, parental choice and teachers' professional development. The chapters in this book were all originally published as articles in Taylor and Francis journals. It is an excellent opportunity to see how others have 'used' Bourdieu's theories.

Forms of capital: general sociology, volume 3: lectures at the Collège de France 1983–4 (2021) Bourdieu P, translated by Peter Collier (Polity)

This book is based on the lectures of Pierre Bourdieu given at the Collège de France in the early 1980s. In these lectures, Bourdieu focuses on one of his critical concepts for which he has become well known: capital. This volume includes Bourdieu's thinking on transmitting cultural capital in the education system and schools.

APPENDIX 3.2

CULTURAL CAPITAL IN REGGIO EMILIA

Reggio Emilia has a unique cultural heritage. It is the birthplace of the tricolour, the national flag of Italy, and other national treasures, such as Parmigiano Reggiano cheese. The city wraps around a busy central piazza, home to a vibrant market, busy coffee shops, cafes and restaurants. Amongst this hive of activity, it is not unusual to observe groups of young children, working purposefully with their teachers or families.

A history of social justice

After the Second World War, with much of Reggio Emilia destroyed by German bombers, a group of working parents set about reclaiming abandoned buildings in the city with the intent of creating a new school system with collaboration at its heart.

The Reggio Emilia Approach®

These days, the name Reggio Emilia is familiar to most early years practitioners wherever they are in the world. While this is predominantly for their child-centred approach to learning, the schools of early childhood have much to teach us about how we can ensure that children's cultural capital is fully valued and nurtured. Here are some things the Reggio Emilia Approach® does that are well worth considering as you develop your curriculum.

Dialogue

Dialogue holds a significant place in the social culture of Reggio Emilia and is central to school and community partnerships.

In the schools, opportunities for conversation are promoted in various ways, including more structured and planned activities and more informal, social interactions. For example, in most settings purpose-built mini piazzas and other open spaces replicate the city's busy piazzas and encourage the casual interactions of city life. Moreover, in the schools' co-constructed curricula, priority is given to dialogue as a means of building children's knowledge and understanding of the world around them.

Family and community engagement

Teachers, families, and the wider community are considered partners, with parents welcomed into schools forming an integral part of the children's learning experience. This extends to shared teacher-parent curriculum planning and parental participation in daily routines, such as baking, cooking, and even gardening of the school grounds. Regular home visits and community engagement enable teachers to learn about each family's existing capital, including, for example, their values, language, traditions and tastes. This deep-rooted collaborative approach gives teachers a real insight into the cultural capital children bring to the school setting and, therefore, can better reflect this in the curriculum and address any gaps or disadvantages the children may have.

Spaces and places

The Reggio Emilia Approach® considers the physical environment as the third teacher. This means that great value is placed on the places and spaces in the school environment including, as already mentioned, purpose-built piazzas. Light also plays an important part of the school environments, with most settings having light-filled open spaces, which encourage the children to socialise and play together. Learning spaces offer children a range of natural materials from the surrounding environment and sustainable materials from local industries with which to play, build, create and explore. The choice of materials helps the children make connections between the local environment, cultural heritage and their place within the world.

Creatively constructed projects

In the Reggio Emilia Approach®, children are encouraged to be curious, building their knowledge about the people, places and events around them. This means that when it comes to the curriculum, the children work alongside their teachers and parents to co-construct projects based on their curiosities, hypotheses and interests. As the children's projects evolve, they explore, investigate, question and experiment, discussing their thoughts and ideas with others. As they do so, children build new knowledge on prior knowledge and often demonstrate a deep understanding of concepts, such as friendship, community and nature. Project work can be incredibly detailed, with children often showing a surprisingly deep understanding, way beyond their years, of the immediate world around them.

Diversity

Reggio Emilia is home to a diverse population with a wide range of cultures, religions, and linguistic backgrounds. This diversity is fostered in and out of the classroom through social interactions between families, the family and the school and in the curriculum with provocations and projects around themes, such as identity and cooperation.

The city also has a rich variety of arts activities and events in which the schools play a fundamental part. Festivals, exhibitions and cultural celebrations all add to Reggio's rich diversity and provide cultural opportunities for the city's children to be involved in the traditions of the city.

The Reggio way

Although there are many reasons why the Reggio Emilia Approach® cannot be replicated in other contexts, there is much to be learned about how primary schools can support nurturing all children's cultural capital. Allowing time for quality dialogue, building good relationships with parents, planning for more involvement in community events, having a flexible and considerate use of space, and building engaging curriculum projects that build deep-rooted knowledge are all things we can realistically achieve.

For a deeper look into the cultural capital of the Reggio Emilia Approach®, it is well worth visiting their website. Furthermore, if you are fortunate to have the opportunity to visit, The Loris Malaguzzi International Centre in Reggio Emilia is an exceptional example of how a city can come together to preserve and grow the cultural traditions, values and experiences of its community and people.

Reference

Reggio Emilia Approach®. Accessed 12 February 2024. https://www.reggiochildren.it/en/reggio-emilia-approach

APPENDIX 3.3

EXAMPLE CULTURAL OFFER

Legend: School · Community · Expert

Year Group	Autumn term 1	Autumn term 2	Spring term 1	Spring term 2	Summer term 1	Summer term 2
Nursery	Family dining day; Librarian story time	'Keeping clean' session with community nurse	Family dining day	Puppet workshop with local theatre group	Family dining day; Library visits	Family summer picnic at local park
Reception		Diwali celebration; Christmas nativity	Chinese New Year lantern parade	Local artist		
Year 1	Parent and child book sharing initiative; Librarian story time	Diwali celebration; Christmas nativity	Chinese New Year lantern parade	Print-making workshop with local artist	Summer book fair	Local history society talk 'How our school has changed over time'

Year 2	Parent and child book sharing initiative / Librarian story time	Diwali celebration / Christmas nativity	Local synagogue visit	Community art exhibition at the local library	Summer book fair	Animal care session at local petting zoo or farm
Year 3	Sculpture workshop with local artist	Christmas carol concert	Library visits	Local history society talk 'How our community has changed over time'	Local mosque visit	Summer book fair and family picnic
Year 4	Urban art visit to local city/ town centre	Christmas carol concert	Library visits		Museum visit	Summer book fair and family picnic

Year 5	Forces lecture with local scientist	Christmas carol concert	Book fair	Space centre visit	Library visits	Local Buddhist temple visit
Year 6	Inheritance and evolution lecture with local scientist	Christmas carol concert	Book fair	Secondary school visits	Year 6 residential (coastal location)	City/town arts festival
	Library visits					Leavers' concert

APPENDIX 5.1

PEDAGOGICAL APPROACHES AND THEIR CHARACTERISTICS

A collaborative pedagogy:

- rejects the notion that children can think, learn and write effectively in isolation
- requires children to engage and collaborate with others and capitalise on each other's knowledge and skills
- uses strategies that are learner centred to maximise critical thinking
- uses strategies that focus on peer-to-peer interaction and interpersonal engagement
- require genuine 'working together' rather than just working in groups
- asks children to use their strengths to help others construct their understanding

A behaviourist pedagogy:

- puts the teacher at the centre of all learning practices
- expects the teacher to lead the lesson
- teaches subject knowledge discretely
- uses strategies, including lecturing, modelling, demonstration and rote learning
- ensures activities are visible and well structured
- requires children to articulate and demonstrate their learning
- is sometimes described as a traditional or formal teaching style

A constructivist pedagogy:

- promotes learning through experiences and reflection
- places the child at the centre of the learning
- encourages play, exploration and enquiry-based learning
- believes children are active rather than passive learners
- requires teachers to focus on how children learn
- uses projects as vehicles for curriculum content
- is sometimes described as progressive
- believes learners are the makers of knowledge and meaning

An enquiry-based pedagogy:

- poses questions, problems or scenarios
- requires the teacher to be a facilitator
- asks learners to identify and research issues and questions to develop their knowledge
- focuses on helping learners acquire the skills necessary to develop their ideas
- uses questions constructively
- asks learners to present their learning to their peers or small groups
- encourages learners to be reflective to determine what did and didn't work
- requires learners to focus on how they learned (metacognition)
- is considered a more progressive than traditional approach to learning

Your pedagogy:

Figure 5.1.1 Pedagogical approaches and their characteristics.

APPENDIX 6.1

EXAMPLE SUBJECT DEVELOPMENT PLAN FOR GEOGRAPHY

Guidance

Priorities	Development activities	Timings	Budget	Success criteria	Monitoring	Outcomes and impact
Break down priorities into clear steps.	Describe the activities that will help achieve each priority.	Map approximate timings, but remember, these should be flexible depending on outcomes.	Plan your costs – even non-contact time is a cost to the school.	Be clear about what you expect the outcomes of your development work to be.	Explain how you will monitor each activity.	Outcomes and impact can be added at a later date.

Geography priority	Development activity	Start date	End date	Cost	Success criteria	Monitoring	Outcomes and impact
Identify strengths and weaknesses of the current geography curriculum.	Talk to staff to gather their opinions, carry out book scrutiny in Reception to Year 6, talk to children and monitor geography planning.	January	February	1 day non-contact (£150)	Clear identification of strengths and areas for development in the geography curriculum.	Lesson observations spring term.	
Improve map work, including reading, interpreting and using maps.	Lead whole school staff meeting on map work. Include knowledge progression and sequencing. Distribute research paper on geography for staff to read.	February	June	Purchase maps, including Ordnance Survey maps and atlases (£500).	The aspect of map work in the geography curriculum, including reading, interpreting and using maps, is clearly planned and well-sequenced across the school. Teachers' knowledge of this area of the curriculum improved and children can use the correct terminology of map work when they answer questions.	Book scrutiny and lesson observations.	

APPENDIX 7.1

BIG IDEAS

What are big ideas?

A big idea is a significant concept that can apply to multiple subjects. Together, big ideas reflect the overarching academic intentions of your curriculum. In some cases schools also refer to the big ideas as the goals or endpoints of their curriculum. That is the larger concepts that children should understand by the time they leave their primary education.

For Wiggins et al., big ideas describe the core concepts of single subjects or disciplines.[1] However, big ideas in this book and most primary schools refer to an 'enduring concept that is not constrained by a particular subject or place in time'.[2] Figure 7.1.1 shows examples of big ideas.

Characteristics of big ideas

Erickson et al. and Wiggins et al. propose interesting thinking about what makes a big idea and provide valuable indicators of their characteristics. The following paragraphs are based on some of their thinking and provide valuable criteria for establishing your own big ideas.

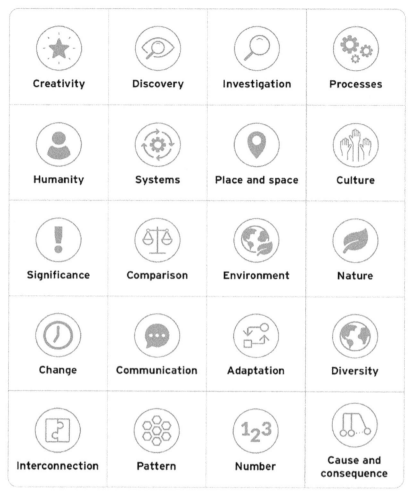

Figure 7.1.1 Example of big ideas.

Big ideas are broad in meaning

Big ideas are sometimes called macro concepts. This is because they are significant concepts that have a broad meaning. Due to their breadth, it's important to have a clear, shared understanding of what each big idea means to you and your stakeholders so there is no room for misunderstanding. Defining your big ideas can be done briefly, as in Figure 7.1.2, or in more detail, as in Figure 7.1.3.

Humankind	**Processes**	**Creativity**	**Investigation**
Understanding what it means to be human and the cause and effect of human behaviour.	Understanding the many dynamic and physical processes that shape the world around us.	Understanding how everyday and exceptional creativity can inspire and change perceptions.	Understanding the importance of asking questions, formulating hypotheses, gathering information and analysing evidence.

Figure 7.1.2 Big ideas with short definitions.

Big ideas are abstract

Big ideas are abstract. That is, they have no concrete form. Therefore, the challenge is bringing those abstractions to life through your curriculum and the lessons teachers teach.

For example, the big idea of creativity can be brought to life in many subjects. For instance, in art and design or design and technology, children can use their creativity to realise their ideas, make objects and find solutions to design problems. Similarly, children can use their creativity in English to write poetry or stories; in science, they may hypothesise and investigate, both of which require creative thinking.

The more opportunities you provide for children to study abstract concepts through meaningful contexts and with specific examples, the better your children will begin to understand how big ideas have meaning in the real world.

Big ideas are timeless

Big ideas are timeless and universal, applicable to any place, race or culture. These concepts will have existed in the past, are relevant in the present and are more than likely to exist in the future. They are steadfast, a fact of life and not at risk of disappearing due to educational, social or political fads or trends.

Humankind

Understanding what it means to be human and the cause and effect of human behaviour.

This big idea invites children to find out what it means to be human, including the workings of human anatomy and how to keep safe. They examine ways that the human race is interconnected and explore the human experience and identities through a range of subject lenses. They discover the cause and effect of human behaviour and develop an understanding of the relationships between individuals, societies, faiths and communities. Through this big idea, children discover the ancient secrets of past civilisations and see the multitude of ways in which they influence modern-day life.

Processes

Understanding the many dynamic and physical processes that shape the world around us.

This big idea invites children to find out about the diverse and dynamic physical processes that are present in, and have a significant impact on, places, the environment and the world around them. They explore the physics of force and movement and investigate the phenomena of electricity, light and sound. Through this big idea, children discover how physical processes, such as weather and erosion, can transform a place or landscape.

Creativity

Understanding how everyday and exceptional creativity can inspire and change perceptions.

This big idea invites children to discover the place of everyday and exceptional creativity, including the qualities of persistence, determination, originality and resilience that form the basis of the creative process. They explore ways in which their ideas and imaginings can be realised and communicated and pursue enquiry by asking questions and finding connections between seemingly separate ideas. Through this big idea, children develop an appreciation of the importance of experimentation, trial and error, original thought and self-expression.

Investigation

Understanding the importance of asking questions, formulating hypotheses, gathering information and analysing evidence.

This big idea invites children to be curious and search for answers in response to original, familiar and more complex questions. They explore ways to create hypotheses, gather evidence and begin to evaluate data. They experiment with different ways to present information and ideas and make informed choices to solve problems. Through this big idea, children start to think critically, make meaningful connections and reflect thoughtfully on evidence and ideas.

Figure 7.1.3 Big ideas with extended definitions.

Big ideas promote primary pedagogy

At a time when the acquisition of knowledge in the curriculum is king, it is a welcome fact that the inclusion of big ideas in a curriculum structure can promote the kind of pedagogy that supports the unique nature of the primary child. Big ideas cannot just be taught and assumed, learned or remembered; they must be uncovered and discovered. Active learning strategies, such as asking questions, investigating hypotheses, making connections and finding patterns, are all important in a curriculum led by big ideas.

Big ideas create meaningful links across the curriculum

One of the most critical functions of big ideas is that they can provide a conceptual lens for different subjects and aspects of the curriculum. For example, take the big idea of nature; there are many ways that this can act as a conceptual lens across numerous subjects. While geography and science might be the obvious place to start, valuable links can be made with other subjects, such as English or art and design. For example, in art and design, children could learn how to draw and paint natural landscapes, with the teacher using the opportunity to revisit the physical features of the landscape. In English, children might write poems about nature, rivers, mountains and the coastline using technical vocabulary they have learned in geography.

It is important to understand that this does not mean looking for tenuous links between subjects but meaningful opportunities for the children to learn and make connections through the lens of a big idea.

Big ideas in maths and English

The subjects of maths and English usually have their own unique big ideas. For example, in English, concepts, such as reading becomes a big idea, as does number in maths.

However, it is still worth reflecting on some of the more universal big ideas in these two subjects where possible, for example, using the big idea of investigation in maths, or comparison in English.

Notes

[1] Wiggins GP, McTighe J. *Understanding by Design*. Merrill/Prentice Hall; 1998.
[2] Erickson HL, Lanning LA, French RL. *Concept-Based Curriculum and Instruction for the Thinking Classroom*. Corwin, a SAGE Publications Company; 2017.

References

Erickson HL, Lanning LA, French RL. *Concept-Based Curriculum and Instruction for the Thinking Classroom*. Corwin, a SAGE Publications Company; 2017.
Wiggins GP, McTighe J. *Understanding by Design*. Merrill/Prentice Hall; 1998.

APPENDIX 7.2

SUBJECT CONCEPTS

What are subject concepts?

Subject concepts are the central ideas of an academic discipline or subject. Unlike big ideas, subject concepts are smaller, more specific and not usually transferable across subjects. However, this rule has some exceptions; for example, the concept of weather can be found in both geography and science.

Purpose of subject concepts

The purpose of subject concepts is two-fold. Firstly, they can help you articulate the essence of each subject, and secondly, they can help you link the big ideas of your curriculum to the teaching and learning that happens in the classroom.

Where a subject concept is multifaceted, it is helpful to consider breaking it down into smaller granular parts, known as aspects. For example, the concept of phenomena in science can be broken down into aspects, such as forces, light and sound. Likewise, in art and design the subject concept of form might be broken down into smaller aspects of 2D and 3D form.

Supporting curriculum coherence

Subject concepts also provide a structural link between the big ideas of your curriculum and the knowledge and skills of your curriculum progression framework.

An example of a structural link is shown in Figure 7.2.1, with the big idea of nature linking to several subject concepts of the curriculum.

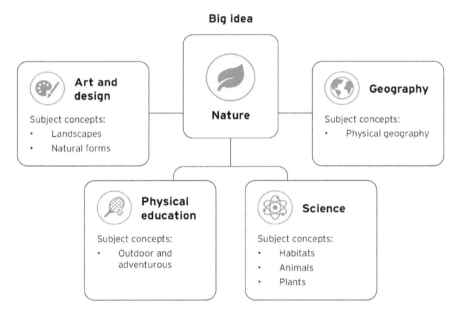

Figure 7.2.1 Structural links between big ideas and subject concepts.

APPENDIX 7.3

CURRICULUM PROGRESSION FRAMEWORK

What is the curriculum progression framework?

Your curriculum progression framework will help you organise the core knowledge – substantive, disciplinary and procedural knowledge – children need to learn to understand your curriculum's subject concepts and big ideas.

Built collaboratively between the subject and curriculum lead, the entire framework comprises individual subject maps, which combine to make one cohesive framework.

The main intention of a curriculum progression framework is to provide an academic structure that will enable children to progress, step by step, towards your curriculum endpoints and goals.

Sequencing

As cognitive load theory suggests, working memory can hold only a small amount of information at any point in time,[1] therefore, the knowledge of your framework must be logically sequenced so as not to overload children's working memories. What's more, it should only reflect the core knowledge of your curriculum. Moving up each year group, the core knowledge in your framework should become more challenging as children build new knowledge on prior knowledge.

While most curriculum frameworks have the basic year-on-year (horizontal) sequencing and within-year (vertical) sequencing resolved, few address the more complex aspects of diagonal sequencing. The following paragraphs highlight some of the different types of sequencing that you will need to consider when creating your curriculum progression framework.

Horizontal sequencing

The content of your framework should be sequenced horizontally so that children know A to understand B. Children who know A and B can use this knowledge and experience to progress to point C. Example in Table 7.3.1.

Table 7.3.1 Horizontal sequencing example

Knowledge	A	B	C
Substantive (facts)	The basic plant parts include root, stem, leaf, flower, petal and fruit.	Plants need water, light and a suitable temperature to grow and stay healthy. Many plants grow from seeds and bulbs.	Roots anchor the plant in the ground and transport water and minerals from the ground to the plant. The stem (or trunk) support the plant above the ground. Leaves collect energy from the Sun and make food for the plant. Flowers make seeds to produce new plants.
Procedural (skills)	Label and describe the basic structure of a variety of common plants.	Describe how plants need water, light and a suitable temperature to grow and stay healthy.	Name and describe the functions of the different parts of flowering plants (roots, stem, leaves and flowers).

Vertical sequencing

Vertical sequencing is the ordering of knowledge within a year group. It is about sequencing lessons so that the knowledge of each subject within the framework is taught and revisited throughout the year and in multiple contexts.

Getting the balance right here is crucial. You do not want your curriculum to be overly repetitive, but you must ensure adequate opportunities for children to revisit learning for retrieval purposes.

Diagonal sequencing

The best curriculum progression frameworks are developed collaboratively between subject leaders so that each subject considers the progression of core knowledge set out in other subjects.

This process is more than ordering each subject's granular parts; it is about the relationship, connection and coherence between subjects. In this book, we'll refer to this as diagonal sequencing. For example, a child needs to know A in geography to understand B in science.

Content

One of the most significant challenges of developing a curriculum progression framework is knowing what knowledge and skills to include. Ultimately, this will depend on your big ideas, subject concepts and what you feel is the core knowledge of each subject.

Ensure you consider the amount of content you include in your framework. On the one hand, it is important to have everything you feel is essential, yet you must be mindful not to overload your framework. Overloading will lead to an overcrowded and impossible-to-cover curriculum. On the other hand, including too few statements can lead to your curriculum becoming too narrow or restricted. Getting the balance right is a fine art that may take time to achieve.

Maths and English

As already highlighted, the subjects of maths and English typically have distinct progression frameworks because they have their own big ideas, subject concepts and core knowledge. Nevertheless, they should be designed in the same way as all other subjects described in this appendix.

Note

[1]   Sweller J. Cognitive load during problem solving: Effects on learning. *Cognitive Science.* 1988; 12: 257–85.

Reference

Sweller J. Cognitive load during problem solving: Effects on learning. *Cognitive Science.* 1988; 12: 257–85.

APPENDIX 7.4

CURRICULUM NARRATIVES

What is a curriculum narrative?

In most primary schools, each subject has its own narrative. The narratives are set out in themes or topics and are usually further embellished by a series of sequenced and well-connected lessons forming projects. These themes, topics and projects then come together to build your whole curriculum narrative.

Content coverage

As part of your subject narratives, you may be required to teach content from a national curriculum; for example, you may have to teach specific historical periods.

If you are not required to teach a national curriculum, you'll have much more freedom to decide on the thematic content you want to include in your narratives. In this case, you should consult other materials, such as non-fiction books and subject-specific websites and consider other factors, such as teacher preferences.

Lessons

Schools sometimes require teachers to create lesson plans as part of their topics or projects. While this is not always done due to workload issues, encouraging teachers to think carefully about the finer details of what they want to teach and in what sequence is often worth doing.

Engagement

Ultimately, your narratives should provide the context, interest and memorable content of your curriculum. It is a chance for each subject to tell its story while teachers can wrap around it the hinterland knowledge that engages and stimulates children's curiosity.

Thinking about your curriculum as a narrative will enable your teachers and subject leaders to think creatively, while ensuring that your curriculum tells a cohesive and interconnected story.

APPENDIX 7.5

CURRICULUM RESOURCES

What are curriculum resources?

Even the most imaginative or resourceful teachers require the right tools for the job. This means having access to the best quality print, practical and digital resources to help them teach and engage children with the curriculum.

Why are resources important?

Curriculum resources give teachers the tools and materials to help children learn. When teachers have an excellent range and quality of teaching resources, they can plan better lessons and provide the best learning experiences for their children. Moreover, with access to quality resources, children are better able and inspired to produce work they can be proud of.

Print-based resources

While some schools decide to create their own resources, others are inclined to purchase commercial resources, such as textbooks. However, these can be restrictive, subject to outdated information due to new knowledge and less likely to be aligned with your bespoke curriculum. There are also many print-based resources to be found online, but these need to be checked thoroughly as they can be of variable quality. For schools that decide to create bespoke resources, this can be a massive undertaking and depends on the expertise of the teaching staff.

As such, many schools look to a hybrid model, choosing commercial schemes for detailed subject-specific support while creating some of their resources bespoke to their curriculum.

Key features of good quality print-based resources include:

- facts and information that are written in an engaging, age-appropriate style
- use of correct and age-appropriate prose, punctuation and grammar
- use of high-quality images, including maps and museum artefacts
- comprehensive use of key terms and vocabulary linked to your curriculum framework
- well-presented, accurate information that is visually appealing
- design features that enhance and do not distract the learner

Digital resources

Digital resources can be a great addition to your curriculum, especially for adding excitement or detail to a lesson. Videos can demonstrate things difficult to grasp in two dimensions, such as blood circulating a body. Apps and other software packages can also bring learning to life and support children with special educational needs.

Physical resources

Physical resources include all the practical equipment and apparatus that children need to carry out the tasks and activities of your curriculum. Such resources can be expensive, so finding creative ways to organise, share and maintain what is available is essential.

Free resources

There is a growth of free resources online. While it is best to avoid resale websites, it is worth investigating organisations, such as the Historical Association,[1] the Geographical Association,[2] and national and local museums and galleries. Many charities also have a selection of free resources, usually of good quality. In many cases, due to the nature of these organisations, the resources are written by experts and are mostly reliable.

Knowledge organisers

A knowledge organiser is a document, usually no more than two sides of A4, that contains key facts and information that children need to have a basic knowledge and understanding of a topic. Most knowledge organisers include knowledge about the topic or theme (usually laid out in easily digestible chunks), technical vocabulary, glossary, data in graphs and charts, quality images, such as maps, diagrams and photographs and additional features, such as a timeline or quotation. It can be hard to know what to include and what to leave out, but creating your own knowledge organisers can help you focus on what you are going to teach and what you want your children to learn.

Notes

[1] History Association. Primary. Accessed 12 February 2024. https://www.history.org.uk/
[2] Geographical Association. Curriculum support. Accessed 12 February 2024. https://geography.org.uk/curriculum-support/geography-subject-leadership-in-primary-and-secondary-schools/

References

Geographical Association. Geography subject leadership. Accessed 12 February 2024. https://geography.org.uk/curriculum-support/geography-subject-leadership-in-primary-and-secondary-schools/
Historical Association. Primary. Accessed 12 February 2024. https://www.history.org.uk/

APPENDIX 7.6

ASSESSMENT

What is assessment?

Assessment and review processes enable you to discover what children do and don't understand. Assessment data can also inform you and your subject leaders about any aspects of the curriculum that are commonly misunderstood and need adapting.

Types of assessment

There are three main forms of assessment. These include:

- assessment for learning – using assessment to provide feedback[1]
- assessment as learning – using assessment to help pupils remember what they have previously learned[1]
- assessment of learning – finding out whether curriculum goals have been achieved[1]

To assess children's learning and the impact of the curriculum, you will need to put each type of assessment in place. This should include considering your position on more formal testing, including any national testing requirements, and the option to purchase more complex assessment systems.

The Independent Commission on Assessment in Primary Education Final Report[2] is a useful document to refer to.

Assessment for and as learning

Assessment for learning and assessment as learning can easily dovetail together to produce quality formative assessment. When built into the curriculum, this type of assessment can provide valuable insight into how your teachers can better help children embed the knowledge of your curriculum.

For example, using skilled questioning at the beginning, during, and end of lessons, as well as low-stakes quizzes, can all help inform, in the short term, what children know and need, rather than as a means of generating scores or levels.

The benefits of using low-stakes quizzes and questioning as a means of assessing what children have learned include:

- reducing children's anxiety
- encouraging children to recall learned knowledge
- reinforcing conceptual understanding
- providing feedback to children about their strengths and weaknesses
- enabling the teacher and child to determine what aspects of the curriculum they might need to revisit or require further explanation
- avoiding placing undue pressure on children to perform at a high level

Assessment of learning

Assessment of learning must be purposeful and provide accurate information about the impact of your curriculum. Assessment of learning is usually done through school-made tests or via online assessment and tracking systems.

In the case of tests, it is important to remember that too much testing can lead to a more stressful experience for children and even a narrowing of the curriculum, as it can lead to an overemphasis on testing rather than teaching.

A test once every half or full term is reasonable and should avoid test fatigue. It is also essential to foster a positive testing culture. For example, using tests as a basis for discussions with children about their learning, sharing their successes and encouraging resilience in those who need it is all part of a reassuring test culture.

Notes

1   Ofsted. Finding the optimum: The science subject report. Published February 2023. Accessed 12 February 2024. https://www.gov.uk/government/publications/subject-report-series-science/finding-the-optimum-the-science-subject-report--2
2   Independent Commission on Assessment in Primary Education. Assessment for children's learning: A new future for primary education. Accessed 12 February 2024. https://www.icape.org.uk/reports/NEU2762_ICAPE_final_report_A4_web_version.pdf

References

Independent Commission on Assessment in Primary Education. Assessment for children's learning: A new future for primary education. Accessed 12 February 2024. https://www.icape.org.uk/reports/NEU2762_ICAPE_final_report_A4_web_version.pdf

Ofsted. Finding the optimum: The science subject report. Published February 2023. Accessed 12 February 2024. https://www.gov.uk/government/publications/subject-report-series-science/finding-the-optimum-the-science-subject-report--2

APPENDIX 7.7

CURRICULUM STRUCTURE

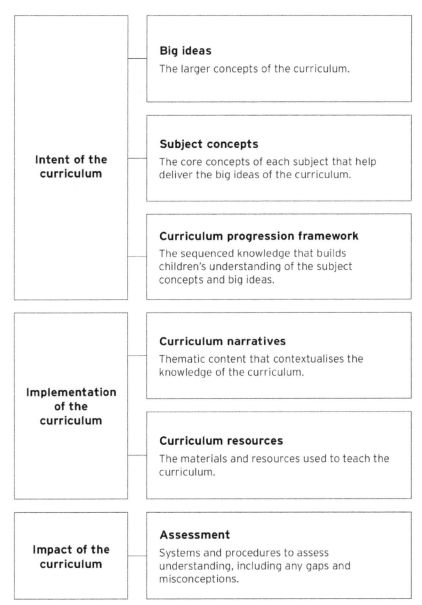

Intent of the curriculum

Big ideas
The larger concepts of the curriculum.

Subject concepts
The core concepts of each subject that help deliver the big ideas of the curriculum.

Curriculum progression framework
The sequenced knowledge that builds children's understanding of the subject concepts and big ideas.

Implementation of the curriculum

Curriculum narratives
Thematic content that contextualises the knowledge of the curriculum.

Curriculum resources
The materials and resources used to teach the curriculum.

Impact of the curriculum

Assessment
Systems and procedures to assess understanding, including any gaps and misconceptions.

Figure 7.7.1 Curriculum structure.

APPENDIX 8.1

CURRICULUM VISION ACTIVITY

Organise your staff into small discussion groups. Photocopy and cut out all the curriculum vision cards in Figures 8.1.1–8.1.3. Each group should have a set of 18 cards. Ask each group to follow the instructions, then discuss their outcomes. Work together to reach a unanimous decision.

Instructions

1. Look at each curriculum vision card.
2. Discuss what each card means to you and your group, and describe what each might look like in practice.
3. Choose your group's most important card and place it on the table.
4. Then choose your group's next two most important cards and place them under the first to begin creating a pyramid, see Figure 8.1.4.
5. Select your group's next three cards and place them below the previous row of cards.
6. Finally, choose four cards to form the base of your pyramid. These four will reflect those that are least important to your group. You can leave out any cards that you feel are not right for your curriculum.

7. Present your ideas to the larger group.
8. Discuss and reflect upon each group's ideas until a unanimous decision is made on which cards you want to guide the design of your curriculum.

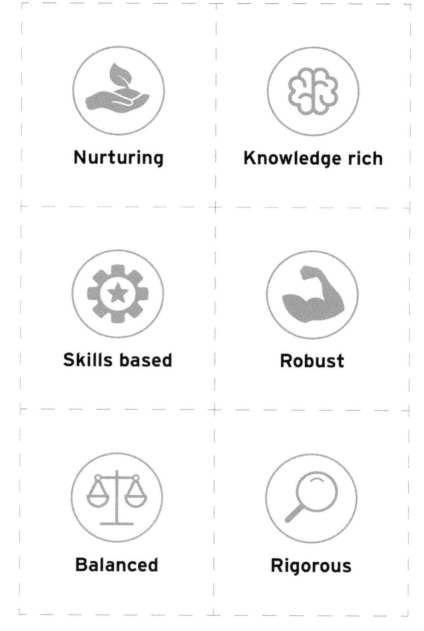

Nurturing

Knowledge rich

Skills based

Robust

Balanced

Rigorous

Figure 8.1.1 Curriculum vision cards – sheet 1.

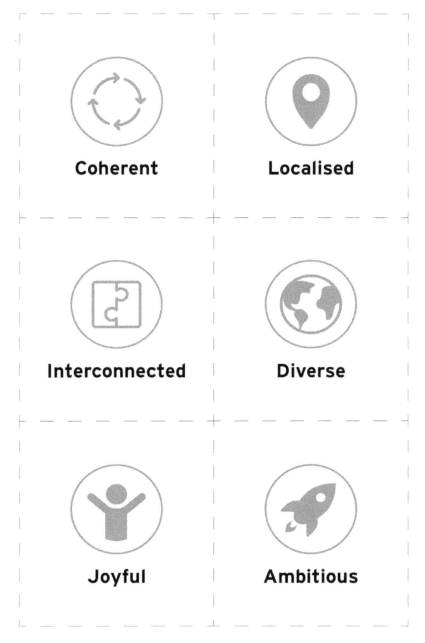

Figure 8.1.2 Curriculum vision cards – sheet 2.

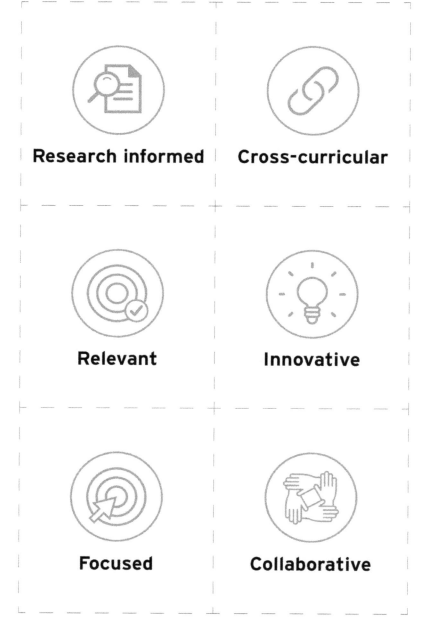

Research informed **Cross-curricular**

Relevant **Innovative**

Focused **Collaborative**

Figure 8.1.3 Curriculum vision cards – sheet 3.

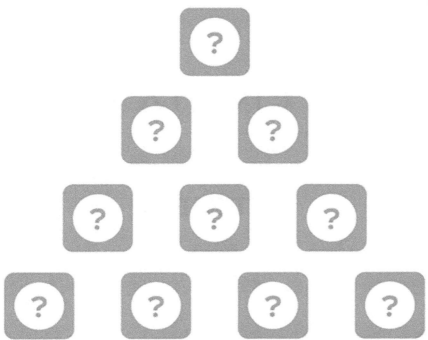

Figure 8.1.4 Vision pyramid.

APPENDIX 8.2

CURRICULUM VISION STATEMENT

Our curriculum aims to provide all children with an equal opportunity to enjoy a high-quality education.

Broad and balanced

Our curriculum values all subjects, so we ensure that all children are taught the nature and truth of each discipline. While maths and English are taught discretely, we also include meaningful opportunities for all our children to apply the knowledge they have learned in maths and English in other subject areas and in a variety of different contexts. By giving our children a broad and balanced curriculum, we aim to help them find the things they are good at and feel passionate about.

Nurturing

Our school is based on a learning community of mutual respect and love. Therefore, our curriculum aims to nurture and develop the whole child. It is inclusive and aims to help all children to succeed, no matter their background or ability. As well as our curriculum being rich in knowledge, we also offer a range of social, emotional and cultural opportunities to help children develop their social and emotional resilience.

Coherent and connected

Our curriculum is well structured and makes explicit connections and links between different subject disciplines. It is purposely designed to maximise opportunities for new learning while including opportunities for retrieval. Subjects and learning experiences are interconnected where appropriate so that key concepts and knowledge are enhanced and revisited in various contexts. This way, we believe our children gain a more three-dimensional understanding of the world around them.

Localised

Our curriculum follows the guidance of the national curriculum. However, it also enables children to learn about their locality, including the people and places around them. We match local studies to aspects of each subject discipline, such as a visit to a local castle for a history project about kings and queens and a regional river study for a geography project. Each year group has at least three local studies as part of their annual curriculum plan.

Diverse

Our curriculum reflects the diverse nature of our local community and our multicultural nation. Children learn about a diverse range of people and places through projects about different cultures, religions and lifestyles, today and throughout history. Throughout the curriculum, we promote the right to share an opinion or point of view and respect each other.

Knowledge rich

Our curriculum is rich in all types of knowledge. This includes substantive knowledge, procedural knowledge and disciplinary knowledge. It is based on a progression framework that sets out a sequenced pathway for children's learning so they can fully understand the key concepts and big ideas of the curriculum.

While we believe children should learn a broad range of knowledge, they should also use and apply it in various contexts. Challenges are set in each curriculum project to allow children to innovate and solve problems. Our curriculum includes well-planned opportunities to retrieve essential knowledge and master its application.

Vocabulary rich

Our curriculum is vocabulary rich and supports our aim to close the gap between word-poor and word-rich households. Each subject has a glossary of critical vocabulary, which forms the foundations of our talk-rich curriculum. This vocabulary starts in the early years and builds progressively across the school. Vocabulary is consistently used across the school in lesson planning and the resources teachers use to support children's learning.

APPENDIX 9.1

CURRICULUM DEVELOPMENT PLAN

Academic year:

Curriculum priority	Development activity	Start date	End date	Cost	Success criteria	Monitoring	Outcomes and impact

APPENDIX 12.1

SUBJECT-SPECIFIC VOCABULARY

In this example, vocabulary is presented as Stage 1 or Stage 2. Stage 1 is for younger children and Stage 2 is for older children. These lists are not exhaustive but give an indication of the type of vocabulary to use in a geography subject map. You can also see that some vocabulary is repeated and revisited across both stages, which supports retrieval practice.

Concept	Stage 1	Stage 2
Human features	Building, capital city, city, country, factory, farm, harbour, house, human-made, landmark, library, office, port, shop, supermarket, town, village	Building, business, canal, city, earthwork, industry, leisure, monument, network, rural, tourism, trade, transport, urban

Concept	Stage 1	Stage 2
Physical features	Beach, cliff, coastline, countryside, desert, forest, hill, landmark, landscape, mountain, ocean, river, sea, seasons, soil, valley, vegetation, weather, woodland	Biome, climate, confluence, deposition, earthquake, erosion, estuary, geology, landscape, mountain, mouth, meander, oxbow lake, plate boundary, plateau, source, tectonic plate, tributary, tundra, vegetation belt, volcano
Fieldwork	Community, compare, conclusion, data, enquiry, feature, graph, local, map, observe, picture, place, record, sketch, space, table, tally	Analysis, chart, conclusion, data, enquiry, environmental, evidence, fieldwork, ground plan, hypothesis, investigation, land use, locality, map, measure, observe, record, region, survey
Mapping	Atlas, compass, direction, position, location, east, feature, globe, key, map, north, picture, route, south, symbol, west	Axis, contour line, coordinate, degree, distance, east, equator, feature, geographical, gradient, grid reference, hemisphere, image, latitude, location, longitude, map, north, north-east, north-west, Ordnance Survey, satellite, scale, south, south-east, south-west, topography, west
Weather and climate	Autumn, cold, cool, dry season, hot, mild, season, spring, summer, temperate, temperature, warm, weather, wet season, winter	Climate, climate zone, desert, drought, equator, flood, heatwave, humid, Mediterranean, polar, rainforest, season, tropical, weather, wildfire

Concept	Stage 1	Stage 2
Location	Earth, continent, country, east, equator, globe, map, north, North Pole, Northern Hemisphere, south, South Pole, Southern Hemisphere, west	Antarctic Circle, Arctic Circle, coordinate, degree, distance, east, latitude, longitude, meridian, north, North Pole, Northern Hemisphere, south, South Pole, Southern Hemisphere, time zone, Tropic of Cancer, Tropic of Capricorn, west
Physical processes	Erosion, material, weathering	Deposition, drainage, earthquake, erosion, plate boundary, precipitation, seismic wave, tectonic plate, transportation, tsunami, volcanic explosion, water cycle
Settlements and land use	City, country, Earth, facility, house, human feature, industry, landmark, locality, office, physical feature, settlement, shop, street, tourism, town, transport, village	Agriculture, arable farming, business, canal, city, commercial, hamlet, land use, leisure, national park, natural resource, pastoral farming, recreational, residential, rural area, settlement, size, town, transport, urban area, village, work
Environment and sustainability	Beach, carbon dioxide, climate change, conservation, damage, deforestation, energy, environment, future, hedgerow, landfill, litter, meadow, pollution, protect, recycle, reduce, reuse, water, woodland	Biodegradable, bioenergy, carbon dioxide, carbon footprint, climate change, conserve, deforestation, depletion, eco-friendly, energy, erosion, fossil fuel, geothermal energy, global warming, habitat, hydroelectric power, non-renewable energy, pollution, recycle, reduce, renewable energy, resource, water, reuse, solar power, sustainable, waste, wildfire, wind power

APPENDIX 12.2

EVALUATING YOUR CURRICULUM PROGRESSION FRAMEWORK

1. Does our curriculum progression framework cover all the necessary concepts and aspects of each subject?
2. Does our curriculum progression framework provide us with all the necessary coverage of any statutory requirements? How do we know?
3. Can we track the journey of one concept horizontally across all year groups?
4. Can we see an increasing amount of challenge from the start to end point of our curriculum?
5. Do our knowledge statements build on prior learning? Can we demonstrate an example to explain how we know?
6. Is our framework manageable? Do we need to increase or decrease its content?
7. Are there areas where we think misconceptions might occur, and how can we support teachers to avoid these pitfalls?

8. Is our framework written with a consistent use of vocabulary? For example, using a verb at the start of procedural knowledge statements.
9. Does each year group feel that the knowledge statements are appropriate for the year group they teach?
10. Are there any changes we want to make before moving onto the next stage of our development work?

APPENDIX 13.1

MEDIUM-TERM PLAN (HALF TERMLY OR TERMLY)

Subject:

Year group	Half term 1	Half term 2	Half term 3	Half term 4	Half term 5	Half term 6
Year 1						
Year 2						
Year 3						
Year 4						
Year 5						
Year 6						

Subject:

Year group	Term 1	Term 2	Term 3
Year 1			
Year 2			
Year 3			
Year 4			
Year 5			
Year 6			

APPENDIX 13.2

DETAILED PROJECT PLAN TEMPLATE

Year group:		Subject:		Project name:		
Big idea	Subject concept/aspect	Vocabulary	Substantive knowledge	Procedural knowledge	Lesson brief (including activities)	

APPENDIX 13.3

EXAMPLE OF INDIVIDUAL PROJECT PLAN

Year group: Year 2   **Subject:** History   **Project name:** Childhood, then and now

Project content/context

A study of how childhood has changed in and beyond living history. This project focuses on the big ideas of comparison, change and investigation and the disciplinary concepts of chronology, same and different and historical enquiry. Children will compare family life and childhood now and in the 1950s. They will use a range of historical artefacts and first- and second-hand sources.

Big idea	Subject concept/aspect	Vocabulary	Substantive knowledge	Procedural knowledge	Lesson brief (including activities)
Change	Chronology	Timeline, before, after, long ago, past, present, then, now	A timeline shows events over a period of time in the order that they happened.	Order information on a timeline.	Ask the children to bring in a range of photographs of themselves as a baby, toddler and as they are now. Ask them to sort their images into chronological order – baby, toddler and child. Provide children with a blank timeline, and ask them to order their photographs on it in the correct sequence. After organising their photographs on the timeline, ask the children to share and compare their timelines with a partner. For those that are able, encourage them to add dates. • Which photograph comes first on your timeline? • Which photographs show the past? • Which photograph shows the present?

Big idea	Subject concept/aspect	Vocabulary	Substantive knowledge	Procedural knowledge	Lesson brief (including activities)
Comparison	Same and different	Same, different, compare, everyday life	Ordinary families in the 1950s had little spare money for treats like holidays. Most homes did not have a television, so people listened to the radio or played board games. Most families did not have a car and travelled by walking, bus or bike.	Describe an aspect of everyday life within or beyond living memory.	Organise the children into small groups and give each group a set of annotated pictures showing aspects of everyday family life in the 1950s. Encourage children to work together to analyse the images and discuss what they show. Invite each group to feed back their findings identifying any similarities and differences between life in the 1950s and today. Allow children to choose a picture to stick in their books and write a sentence about it. • What similarities can you see between life in the 1950s and life today? • What differences can you see between everyday life in the 1950s and life today? • Do you think you'd prefer to live now or in the 1950s? Why?

Big idea	Subject concept/aspect	Vocabulary	Substantive knowledge	Procedural knowledge	Lesson brief (including activities)
Comparison	Same and different	Childhood, school, same, different	In schools in the 1950s, reading, writing and arithmetic, called the Three 'Rs', were very important. Times tables were learned by chanting aloud. Children in the 1950s did not have computers or other technology in their classrooms like children do today.	Describe an aspect of everyday life within or beyond living memory.	Recap what children have learned so far about life in the 1950s by asking questions. Explain that they are going to investigate schools in the 1950s by using old photographs. Model how to use the photographs to look for clues and gather evidence. Demonstrate how to record their observations on a prepared recording sheet. Encourage the children to share and discuss their findings. Work together to summarise key learning points, and identify how schools in the 1950s were similar to or different from schools today. • What were the daily routines of a 1950s classroom? • How are they the same or different from today? • Would you have liked to go to school in the 1950s? Why?

Big idea	Subject concept/aspect	Vocabulary	Substantive knowledge	Procedural knowledge	Lesson brief (including activities)
Significance	Significant events	Coronation, queen, king, reign, celebration, monarch, monarchy	The coronation of Queen Elizabeth II took place on 2 June 1953 at Westminster Abbey in London. The coronation of King Charles III and Queen Camilla took place on 6 May 2023 at Westminster Abbey in London. Charles acceded the throne on 8 September 2022 due to the death of his mother, Elizabeth II.	Identify some key features of a significant historical event within living memory.	Display pictures showing the coronation of Queen Elizabeth II and ask the children to describe what they think the images show, drawing their attention to the dates. Explain the significance of the pictures and the importance of Queen Elizabeth II (1926–2022). Explain that the coronation was the start of the Queen's reign as monarch. Challenge the children to choose one image to draw and describe what is happening using full sentences. Extend by showing children images or footage of King Charles III coronation, and use questions to make comparisons with the coronation of Queen Elizabeth II. • Who was Queen Elizabeth II? • Why was she important? • What is a coronation? • Why was this historical event important? • Would you have liked to attend the coronation? Why?

Big idea	Subject concept/aspect	Vocabulary	Substantive knowledge	Procedural knowledge	Lesson brief (including activities)
Investigation	Historical enquiry	Past, present, same, different, compare	Popular toys of the 1950s included dolls, rocking horses, wooden blocks, train sets, skipping ropes and board games. Most toys required children to use their imaginations. In the 1950s children did not have many toys, and there were no technological toys, such as radio-controlled cars or game consoles.	Use historical artefacts and first-hand and second-hand sources to identify similarities and differences between aspects of everyday life now and in the past.	Introduce the historical enquiry 'What were toys like in the 1950s?' Provide a set of 'then and now' picture packs. Model how to describe and compare toys from the past with toys from the present day, focusing on factors, such as technology, materials and functionality. Ask children to use the images to gather their thoughts and answer the enquiry question. Allow the children to feedback verbally to the group. • What were toys made from in the 1950s? • Are the materials used the same or different from modern toys? Why might they be different? • Which toys would you rather play with? Why? • What conclusions did you draw from the evidence to explain what toys were like in the 1950s?

APPENDIX 13.4

EVALUATING YOUR SUBJECT NARRATIVES

1. Is there a good range of [subject] projects across the school?
2. Do the projects provide a good [subject] narrative over time?
3. Are the projects in the correct order? Do they enable children to build new knowledge on prior knowledge?
4. Are there any gaps in the narrative? What is missing?
5. How could any gaps be addressed?
6. Are the projects equally ambitious?
7. Are the big ideas reflected in the projects?
8. Do the planned activities help deliver the concepts, aspects and knowledge of the curriculum progression framework?
9. Does the project fit with the local or national cycle of events? For example, religious celebrations, cultural events, residentials, specialist curriculum weeks, etc.
10. What adaptations are needed before moving on to the next steps?

APPENDIX 14.1

KNOWLEDGE ORGANISERS

What is a knowledge organiser?

A knowledge organiser is an integral part of a knowledge-rich and ambitious curriculum, a tool used to establish and present the core knowledge of a curriculum project.

Features of knowledge organisers

Although schools can take very different approaches to developing their knowledge organisers, there are some standard features. These include:

- core knowledge and contextual information (hinterland knowledge) about a topic
- images, including maps, diagrams and photographs
- data in graphs, tables and charts
- the use of headings and subheadings to break up information
- subject-specific vocabulary related to the project

- a glossary of key terms
- organisational tools, such as timelines and diagrams.

Style

Knowledge organisers can vary enormously in style and quality. Therefore, it is vital to decide your non-negotiable standards. You will also need to confirm how you expect teachers and children to use the knowledge organisers so there is consistent practice across the school.

Lengthwise, most knowledge organisers tend to fill one to two sides of A4 and use the space effectively not to overwhelm the children with too much information. The look of the knowledge organiser is also a factor in how desirable it is to read.

A combination of core knowledge, with some contextual prose and other valuable features, such as maps, diagrams, quality photographs, timelines and glossaries, is the most appropriate style for primary-aged children.

How to use knowledge organisers

Knowledge organisers can be used in various ways. This can include as a starting point for a project, a home learning resource for parents and carers, and a point of reference for children throughout a project. In some cases, children might want to annotate their knowledge organisers as they progress through the project, adding bits of information to expand their understanding. Older children can use them as a model for making their own knowledge organisers.

Knowledge organisers can also be used in other valuable ways:

- To generate questions about a project
- As a retrieval tool alongside low-stakes quizzes
- To identify gaps in children's knowledge
- As a focus for a learning display
- To strengthen teacher knowledge
- As a focus for group or guided reading or discussion
- As a project-specific spelling and vocabulary reminder
- For older children to revisit or expand their understanding of key-words or themes using a framework such as the Frayer Model.[1]

Benefits

There are many benefits of using knowledge organisers. In the first instance, I have always found them to be a great way to introduce a new project – giving children a sense of the bigger picture and enthusing them about their up-and-coming learning.

Moreover, some curriculum themes can be complicated, so having the knowledge for that project all in one place and presented succinctly can act as a handy tool for children to use as a reference to recall learned knowledge.

Making knowledge organisers part of a display that children can access is a great way of encouraging them to check or recall something without them asking the teacher. This is also a valuable way to develop children's confidence and independence.

Another benefit of having knowledge organisers available is that if a child misses a lesson, they have a point of reference for any knowledge they have missed.

Pitfalls

As with any teaching resource, there are pitfalls to knowledge organisers – mainly around the way they are used. Here are some of the main issues and how to avoid them.

First and foremost, it is essential to remember that knowledge organisers are a valuable tool in your armoury but should not be used as an end in themselves. The body of knowledge that children gain at the end of a topic or project should be deeper and broader than what is outlined by the knowledge organiser. Refer back to hinterland knowledge in Chapter 2 for reference.

Make sure that your knowledge organisers are age-appropriate. They must meet age-related expectations and national curriculum programmes of study if relevant to your school. They should be engaging, clear resources that children trust and use regularly.

Some children may need other ways of using knowledge organisers. You can record audio versions for those who may struggle with reading levels.

Make sure you use copyright-free and quality images – using poor images can lead to misconceptions in children's learning, and using images without copyright permission can get you into hot water, especially if you publish them on your school website.

Finally, including everything on a knowledge organiser could give the game away before a project has even begun. You'll need to decide which facts are spoilers and which will encourage curiosity.

Knowledge organisers can be incredibly useful and versatile when written, designed and used well. However, they should never be relied upon as the be-all and end-all of children's learning, as this can be pretty restrictive, especially for primary children.

Note

[1] Frayer DA, Fredrick WC, Klausmeier HJ. *A Schema for Testing the Level of Concept Mastery: Report from the Project on Situational Variables and Efficiency of Concept Learning.* Wisconsin Research and Development Center for Cognitive Learning; 1969.

Reference

Frayer DA, Fredrick WC, Klausmeier HJ. *A Schema for Testing the Level of Concept Mastery: Report from the Project on Situational Variables and Efficiency of Concept Learning.* Wisconsin Research and Development Center for Cognitive Learning; 1969.

APPENDIX 14.2

KNOWLEDGE ORGANISER PLANNING TEMPLATE

Project title	Images, tables, diagrams and illustrations

Core knowledge

Contextual (hinterland) knowledge

Key vocabulary

Quotes

Timelines/Charts/etc

Figure 14.2.1 Knowledge organiser planning template.

APPENDIX 14.3

EXAMPLE KNOWLEDGE ORGANISERS

Ammonite

What is an ammonite?

Ammonites were sea creatures that lived millions of years ago. Ammonites are an excellent subject matter for drawing and printmaking as they have a distinct shape and pattern.

Drawing pencils

Pencil is an excellent medium for drawing. Pencils can be hard or soft. A soft pencil is best for shading. A hard pencil is best for fine lines and details. An HB pencil is best for sketching as it is a medium grade pencil.

soft

hard

HB

Sketches

Many artists are inspired by natural forms. This sketch by artist Dale French captures the fossils' unique lines, patterns and shape. The artist has used techniques such as shading and cross hatching to give the drawing a sense of form.

Drawing techniques

Artists use a variety of drawing techniques to create tone, texture and form in their work.

Hatching: Parallel lines in one direction.

Cross-hatching: Lines that cross over each other.

Shading: The darkening of a drawing with lines or blocks of colour.

Motifs

A motif is a symbol or simplified shape used in printmaking. Shells are excellent subject matter for creating a motif. This is because they usually have a strong shape or pattern.

Glossary

form	The 3-D aspect of a piece of artwork.
medium	The materials used by an artist.
parallel	Being equal distance apart and never meeting.
pattern	A decorative design that is repeated.
texture	The way a surface or substance feels or looks.

Figure 14.3.1 Year 2 example knowledge organiser.

Food for Life

Processed food

Processed food is any food that has been changed during its preparation. Foods can be altered in different ways, including drying, baking, pasteurising, freezing, canning, washing, cutting, heating or filtering.

Foods can be categorised according to how much they have been processed.

- **Unprocessed** foods are whole foods that have not been changed.

- **Minimally-processed** foods have been changed slightly, for example, by packaging or cutting.

- **Processed** foods that have had ingredients added.

- **Ultra-processed** foods have had artificial ingredients added and have been changed in other ways.

Whole foods

Whole foods are foods that have not been changed from their natural form. These include many fruits and vegetables and some meats and fish. Whole foods contain nutrients important in a healthy, balanced diet. Some whole foods are organic, meaning they are grown or reared without synthetic fertilisers, pesticides or animal feed additives.

Food labels

Food labels can inform consumers about a food's nutritional value. Colour-coded labelling shows the amount of fat, saturated fat, sugar and salt in the food and what percentage of the recommended daily intake each serving contains.

Glossary

additives	Ingredients added to foods such as flavouring and colouring.
shelf life	The length of time a food product can be kept and remain usable.
yeast	A simple organism used to make bread rise.

	Advantages	Disadvantages
Processed food	• convenient • long shelf life • available all year round	• reduced nutritional value • can be high in fats, salt and sugar • can contribute to an unhealthy lifestyle
Whole food	• minimal processing • high in nutrients • contributes to a healthy lifestyle	• can take time to prepare and cook • shorter shelf life

Figure 14.3.2 Year 4 example knowledge organiser.

APPENDIX 15.1

EXAMPLE SCIENCE QUIZZES

Year 6: Light quiz

Tick each statement to show if it is true or false.

Statements	True	False
1. Light can be natural or artificial.		
2. Light is reflected from dull surfaces.		
3. Light is absorbed by shiny surfaces.		
4. The sun is a reflector.		
5. Shadows are formed when an object blocks the passage of light.		
6. Light from the sun contains harmful ultraviolet rays.		
7. Light travels in curved lines.		
8. Light enters the eye through the pupil.		

Additional challenge
Where the statement is incorrect, write the correct statement in the box below.

Year 4: Sound quiz

Questions
1. Complete this sentence: Sound is _____ that travels in _____ from a source through a _____ to our ears.
2. Circle the correct words to complete these sentences about volume and pitch. The harder an instrument is struck, plucked or blown, the **quieter/louder** the volume. The softer an instrument is struck, plucked or blown, the **quieter/louder** the volume. The longer a string or column of air, the **higher/lower** the pitch. The shorter a string or column of air, the **higher/lower** the pitch. The thicker a string, the **higher/lower** the pitch. The thinner a string, the **higher/lower** the pitch. The tighter a string, the **higher/lower** the pitch. The looser a string, the **higher/lower** the pitch. Fast vibrations produce **high-pitched/low-pitched** sounds.
3. Number these statements in order from 1 to 4 to describe how a sound source creates sound waves. Number: .... The nearby air particles then start to vibrate and collide with the air particles ....next to them. Number: .... As the vibrating sound source moves, it collides with particles of air that are .... close by. Number: .... The air particles pass the vibration energy along in waves. Number: .... When energy is put into a sound source, it starts to vibrate.

APPENDIX 15.2

TEST STYLE QUESTIONS FOR SCIENCE

Examples of shorter and more extended questions

- Shorter question: What is a producer, and what is a consumer?
- Extended question: Describe what would happen within a habitat if there was an increase in the consumer population.
- Shorter question: What are the four stages of the water cycle?
- Extended question: Explain how temperature controls the water cycle. Use labelled diagrams in your answer.

Examples of labelling questions

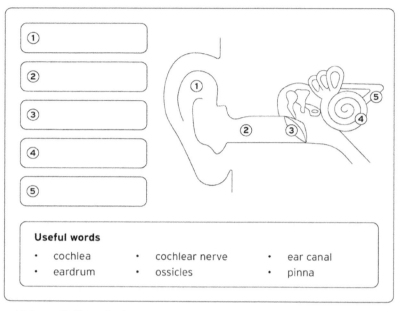

①

②

③

④

⑤

Useful words
- cochlea
- cochlear nerve
- ear canal
- eardrum
- ossicles
- pinna

Figure 15.2.1 Labelling the human ear.

1.
2. mandible
3. humerus
4. rib
5.
6.
7.
8. radius
9.
10. patella
11.
12. fibula

Useful words
- cranium
- femur
- pelvis
- spine
- tibia
- ulna

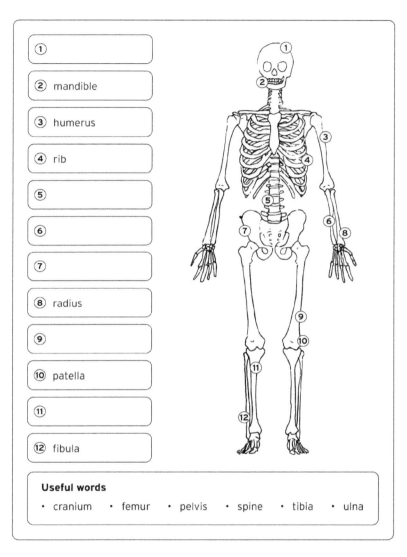

Figure 15.2.2 Labelling the human skeleton.

Matching

cochlea	The tiny bones that transfer vibrations from the middle ear to the inner ear.
cochlear nerve	The tightly stretched skin inside the ear that vibrates when sound waves reach it.
ear canal	The external part of the ear that funnels sound waves into the ear canal.
eardrum	The tube that leads from the outer to the inner ear.
ossicles	The spiral-shaped part where tiny hairs vibrate.
pinna	The part that sends electrical signals to the brain, which interprets them as sounds.

Figure 15.2.3 Matching ear parts and functions.

Tables and charts

Animal parts quiz Y3

Tick whether each statement is true or false. For false statements, explain why it is false.

Statement	True	False	Reason why if false
Humans are omnivores because they can eat plants and animal meat.			
Humans can eat anything they want and still be healthy.			
Vitamins and minerals are not needed in a healthy diet.			

Factual, concept and opinion-based questioning

Type of question	Example
Factual recall	How do…? Why did…? Why do…? How many…? What is the…?
Concept based	How are X and Y connected? What is another way to express X? What will happen if…? What are the consequences of…? What is the impact of…?
Opinion based	Why do you think? What, in your view…? How would you explain? Why do you think…?

APPENDIX 16.1

MONITORING TEMPLATES

Curriculum leader monitoring sheet

Area	Monitoring questions Lines of enquiry	Monitoring activity (e.g. planning scrutiny, book scrutiny, lesson observations, discussions)	Evidence What evidence do you see? What are your judgements against the monitoring questions?
Planning	Does the teacher's short-term planning match the medium- and long-term planning for [subject]?		
Teaching	Does the teaching of [subject/s] align with our intended curriculum?		

Actual curriculum	What areas of [subject] are well taught? Which needs improvement?		
	Are the big ideas of (subject) evident in children's books?		
	Do children demonstrate an understanding of disciplinary concepts in [subject/s]?		
	Are there any emerging misconceptions?		
	What are the emerging strengths of [subject]?		
	What are the areas of [subject] that need development?		
	Is progress evident across school?		
	Are children able to retain the knowledge taught? How do we know?		
	Are children motivated in [subject]?		
Other	What evidence is there that progress and attainment are measured?		
	Where is the evidence of children's personal development through [subject]?		
	Is [subject] helping to develop children's cultural capital?		

SWOT analysis

Strengths What parts of our curriculum are having a positive impact on children's learning?		**Weaknesses** What parts of our curriculum are not having a positive impact on children's learning?	
Opportunities What are the opportunities for improvement?		**Threats** What challenges do we need to address in to improve our curriculum?	

Work sampling/book looks

Monitoring questions	Evidence
What is the main concept/subject/aspect of the curriculum being monitored?	
What evidence is there that [concept/subject/aspect] is being taught well?	
Based on children's work, is there a sufficient challenge in teaching activities?	
Is there evidence of [concept/subject/aspect] developing over time?	
Is there any evidence of misconceptions? If so, what are they?	
Are the resources in use supporting children's learning of [concept/subject/aspect]? Explain your thinking?	
Summary notes (including children's comments)	

Interviews/Conferencing

Focus	Teaching staff	Children
Concepts or aspects	Which disciplinary concepts/aspects have you been focusing on this term? Which concepts/aspects do you think fit our curriculum well? Which concepts/aspects have children struggled with? Why?	Which concepts/aspects have you been learning about this term? Which of the big ideas have you been learning about? Can you explain the concept/big ideas of X?
Subjects	Which subjects are you confident to teach? Does our curriculum support you to teach this subject? How well do you think children are learning the key ideas of [subject]?	Which subjects have you been focusing on this term? What have you learned? Can you tell me why [subject] is important?
Content	Which topics and projects have you taught this term? How well does the content support the children's understanding of this topic? What changes would you make to better support children's learning?	Which projects have you done this term? What can you remember about this project? Did this project inspire you to want to know more about [topic]?
Activities	Do the activities in this project support all children's learning? How well do the activities and resources support children's learning?	Which activities did you enjoy? What did they help you to do/understand? What was the purpose of this activity?

Learning	What concepts/aspects of the curriculum have children learned well? Are there any misconceptions arising in this topic? What are they? Are children making progress? Are there any emerging gaps in this concept/aspect of the curriculum? How would you describe children's achievements?	What do you know now that you didn't know before? What can you do now that you couldn't do before? What do you think you need to revisit? Do you think you've made good progress this term? How do you know?
Engagement	Are children engaging well with our new curriculum? Are children enjoying their learning? Do children feel positive about their learning?	How do you feel about our new curriculum? What would you like to do more of? Do you think the resources are helping you to learn?
Views and experience	What are your experiences of this new/adapted curriculum? Would you like to make any other comments or suggestions about the curriculum going forwards?	What else would you like to tell me about our new curriculum?

APPENDIX 16.2

HISTORY SUBJECT LEADER'S REPORT

This report comes after a full academic year of our new history curriculum. It is based on evidence from a series of monitoring activities carried out by Mr. Smith, the subject leader for history.

Quality of learning

Book looks have demonstrated that history is being well taught across the school and that children are developing their understanding of key historical concepts, such as significance and chronology. Evidence shows that teachers use their medium-term planning to focus on the pertinent concepts of the curriculum and design activities and resources that support and enhance children's learning. Where children find the curriculum challenging, children's books show that teachers have supported them with one-to-one or peer support. Scaffolding resources are also used well to help children access more difficult concepts.

The concept of cause and consequence is less well addressed in teachers' planning and, therefore, in children's learning. When asked in discussions,

Year 2 and Year 5 children could not articulate the meaning of this concept, and so, more work needs to be done on this next year.

Teachers are becoming highly skilled at adapting the planned curriculum where needed and recording these changes, which will help us to make these changes to our curriculum progression framework.

Overall, children make steady, measured progress and are confident in sharing their new knowledge.

Curriculum coherence and multidisciplinary links

Through book looks and the analysis of teachers' planning, it is evident that the curriculum progression framework is enabling teachers and children to make meaningful links across the curriculum to enhance their understanding of multidisciplinary concepts. For example, in history, children draw on their understanding of democracy in Greek history to appreciate the importance of rule of law and democracy in the modern age, as part of their studies of spiritual, moral, social and cultural development. Moreover, teachers have also worked hard to enhance children's cultural capital through the study of local history, including visits to regional historical sites and monuments.

Resources

Artefact boxes have been created for some history projects, and teachers are finding these helpful for the study of first- and second-hand evidence. These resources will need to continue to be developed to help us improve this aspect of the history curriculum and acknowledge that this will have to be gradual due to budgetary restrictions. Our print-based resources are working well, but teachers have expressed a need for more historical information books and stories related to historical topics to encourage reading across the curriculum and as an additional source of historical information.

Strengths in history

There is an enthusiasm demonstrated by staff and children for our history curriculum. Children enjoy engaging topics and teachers are feeling more confident in teaching the subject. Aspects of our whole school pedagogy, such as the asking of questions and the process of enquiry, help teachers to teach the procedural knowledge of history.

Other strengths observed include robust lesson planning and effective sequencing, which is based on our history progression map and is evident in book looks across school.

Future developments

- Staff development and training on how to teach concepts of cause and consequence.
- Continue to develop the use of first- and second-hand evidence by expansion of history artefact boxes.
- Continue to maximise interdisciplinary links between history and other subjects.
- Improve children's access to historical non-fiction and fiction texts.

GLOSSARY

actual curriculum   The curriculum that is taught.

aspects   The smaller parts of a multifaceted subject concept.

big ideas   Large concepts that are broad in meaning, abstract in nature and often capable of being applied to multiple subjects. Sometimes referred to as a macro concept.

cognitive load theory (CLT)   The idea that our working memory can only manage a limited amount of information at one time (Sweller.J). There are two types of cognitive load:
Intrinsic: the inherent difficulty of the material.
Extraneous: the load generated by how the material is presented.

broad and balanced curriculum   A curriculum approach that values and teaches all subjects.

cross-curricular   A way of organising learning so that different subjects are taught connectedly.

cultural capital (in education)   The provision of cultural experiences, knowledge and skills. There are three types of cultural capital: Embodied, Institutionalised and Objectified.

cultural capital (embodied)   Embodied cultural capital refers to knowledge or skills that a person acquires from his/her habitus. Examples include routines, accents, etiquette, and a robust vocabulary.

cultural capital (institutionalised)   Institutionalised capital is the recognition of a person's cultural capital, by formal educational institutions. It includes academic credentials, professional qualifications and awards.

cultural capital (objectified)   Objectified cultural capital is the value inherent in objects of culture, such as works of art. For the possession of the artwork to constitute objectified cultural capital, the individual must be knowledgeable about its historical, cultural and aesthetic significance.

cultural capital (theory)   The familial transmission of capital to a child that occurs without intent, including social and psychological constructs, such as language, mannerisms and tastes.

cultural offer   The cultural experiences offered by a school.

curriculum leader   The person in school that leads the school's curriculum development and improvement.

curriculum principles   The parameters by which a school designs its curriculum, for example, knowledge rich or enquiry led.

curriculum narrative   How single or multiple subjects are mapped across the curriculum to form a narrative.

curriculum progression framework   A means of sequencing the core knowledge that children need to learn at each key stage in order to understand the subject concepts, aspects and big ideas of the school curriculum.

diagonal sequencing   The ordering of knowledge across subjects.

disciplinary knowledge   The particular techniques and methodologies by which the substantive knowledge of a subject is acquired or proven.

early years curriculum   A school curriculum for very young children, usually aged from three to five years old.

governor   A person who oversees the educational and financial performance of the school and supports the headteacher with strategic direction.

habitus   A set of norms and expectations unconsciously acquired by a person through experience and socialisation of the family. In simple terms, those things that are second nature to an individual or a 'way of being'.

hidden curriculum   The knowledge children acquire which is often unplanned.

hinterland knowledge   The extra contextual knowledge children need to understand subject concepts or vocabulary.

horizontal sequencing   The ordering of knowledge across all year groups in the curriculum progression framework.

intended curriculum   The curriculum a school plans to teach, usually set out in a curriculum progression framework.

key vocabulary   The specific words that are integral to a child's understanding of the topic or subject.

knowledge-rich curriculum   A curriculum approach that puts an emphasis on the teaching of academic knowledge.

knowledge organiser   A curriculum resource that contains core and sometimes contextual knowledge of a topic or project.

learned curriculum   The knowledge, skills, attitudes and behaviours children learn as a result of being taught the intended curriculum.

localisation   A process that integrates local people, places and resources into the curriculum to enhance children's learning.

monitoring   The activities used to gather information about the impact of the curriculum.

national curriculum   A set of government statutory requirements for subject coverage and expected standards.

pedagogy   How the school curriculum is taught.

Pierre Bourdieu (1930–2002)   French sociologist and public intellectual who first coined the phrase 'cultural capital'.

practical resources   The physical equipment used by teachers and learners.

procedural knowledge   The specific actions performed within a particular subject to gain or use substantive knowledge. More commonly referred to as skills.

programme of study   A government document which outlines the required coverage for a specific subject.

Reggio Emilia Approach®   A branded, child-centered pedagogical approach to early years education developed in Reggio Emilia, Italy.

retrieval (practice)   A pedagogic strategy which requires the learner to bring to mind previously learned knowledge in order to boost learning.

Rosenshine principles   A branded pedagogical approach to teaching developed by Professor Barak Rosenshine (1930–2017). Focuses on methods of facilitating knowledge acquisition and recall.

schema   A cognitive structure that helps us understand how things work.

sequencing   The process of mapping out something in a particular order. For example, mapping knowledge in the curriculum progression framework so that new knowledge builds on prior knowledge.

skills   The specific actions used within a particular subject to gain or use substantive knowledge. Also referred to as procedural knowledge.

social justice   A principle maintaining that all people in a society should have equal rights, opportunities, and treatment.

stakeholder   A person, group or organisation with a vested interest in the school.

subject leader   A person who establishes the strategic aims for the subject they lead; assesses, monitors and evaluates the effectiveness of teaching and learning in the subject; adapts the curriculum accordingly and provides teachers with the necessary resources to effectively implement their plans.

subject map   The mapping of a subject's concepts and knowledge in relation to the big ideas of the school curriculum.

subject narrative   The 'story' used to deliver curriculum content. Usually organised into a sequenced blocks called projects or topics.

substantive knowledge   Facts about the places, people, events and processes of the world.

vertical sequencing   The ordering of knowledge within a year group.

vision statement   A statement to help a school set out the goals and ambitions for its curriculum.

INDEX

Note: **Bold** page numbers refer to tables; *italic* page numbers refer to figures and page numbers followed by "n" denote endnotes.

9 781032 781792